KU-496-095

# Contents

KEY TO MAPS

✈ Airport

★ Start of walk/drive

229m ▲ Mountain

ℹ Information

† Church

A6 Road No.

## Maps

## Features

## Walks and Tours

# Introduction

A colourful past and age-old traditions combine with an abundance of scenic beauty and natural resources to make Lithuania a fascinating and rewarding destination for all travellers. For a moderately sized country, it packs in a variety of experiences and many welcome surprises. Lithuania offers it all – places of varied interest, medieval towns steeped in history and culture, a slew of national parks, superb landscapes that offer great driving routes and walks and, for the more energetic, opportunities for sporting activities, as well as places to go for relaxed swims or simply lie in the sun.

A beach on the Curonian Spit

The three largest cities of Lithuania – the capital Vilnius, the old capital Kaunas, and Klaipėda, a strategic port on the Baltic Sea – are all interesting places, steeped in history. Simply wandering around the streets is like embarking on a lesson in the

development of European architecture, with examples from as early as the 13th century, through the Gothic, baroque and Renaissance eras, to the ultra-modern. Museums and galleries are aplenty, particularly in Vilnius, which has enough to keep you busy for many days. Evening entertainment in the cities ranges from the sophisticated to folksy traditions in music.

Travellers who consider retail therapy an essential part of a holiday will not be disappointed by the shopping options either. Vilnius and Kaunas, as well as Šiaulių in the north, have excellent shops with many of the European chain stores represented. Local specialities such as amber and high-quality craft items are widely available as well.

If relaxation is what you are after, there's a lot of choice: sun, sea and sand – sea and sand guaranteed – can be found in abundance along Lithuania's Baltic coast. The extraordinary natural phenomenon of the Curonian Spit –

# LITHUANIA

BY

POLLY PHILLIMORE AND LINDARA KIELY

Produced by
Thomas Cook Publishing

**Written by** Polly Phillimore and Lindara Kiely
**Photography by** Polly Phillimore

Edited and designed by Laburnum Technologies Pvt Ltd,
C-533 Triveni Apts, Sheikh Sarai Phase 1,
New Delhi 110017

Published by Thomas Cook Publishing
A division of Thomas Cook Tour Operations Limited

PO Box 227, Unit 18, Coningsby Road,
Peterborough PE3 8SB, United Kingdom
E-mail: books@thomascook.com
www.thomascookpublishing.com
Tel: +44 (0) 1733 416477

ISBN13: 978-1-84157-579-7
ISBN10: 1-84157-579-8

Text © 2006 Thomas Cook Publishing
Maps © 2006 Thomas Cook Publishing

First edition © 2006 Thomas Cook Publishing

Project Editor: Linda Bass
Production / DTP Editor: Steven Collins

Printed and bound in Spain by: Grafo Industrias Graficas, Basauri

Cover design by: Liz Lyons Design, Oxford
Front cover credits: Left © Glen Allison / Getty Images; Centre ©
Lebrecht Music and Arts Photo Library / Alamy; Right © Jon Arnold
Images / Alamy.
Back cover credits: Left © Andrew Jankunas / Alamy; Centre © AllOver
Photography / Alamy

now Neringa National Park – encapsulates sand dunes, beaches and pine forests. Swim, sunbathe or simply take a walk through the woods.

Just north of Klaipėda, situated on this stretch of coast, are other small resorts leading up to Palanga, Lithuania's premier seaside resort. Here you can enjoy dunes and sandy beaches side by side with the beautiful botanical gardens. Palanga is a busy, thriving town with all the attractions of a highly popular seaside resort; it is also known as a health resort, with several hotels offering specialised treatments.

However, if it is a spa holiday you are really after, Druskininkai, in the south of Lithuania, is the place for you. One of the earliest spa centres in Europe, it has a wonderful microclimate, scenic beauty and all the treatments you could possibly want.

There are plenty of places where one can enjoy Lithuania's fabulous natural wealth of lakes and forests, its landscapes of gentle hills and fertile plains. The country boasts five national parks and numerous regional parks. Aside from spearheading conservation efforts, these offer a range of activities from walks to boating to birdwatching. Stay in and around the parks to immerse yourself in the tradition and culture of these areas, even as you revel in their diversity.

This will gladden the heart of the traveller who likes to keep on the move – the country's transport infrastructure is excellent. Routes are well signposted and getting from one place to another is pretty much hassle-free.

The Lithuanians are a friendly, hospitable people and English is widely spoken. Their love of the country is readily apparent, and they are proud to help you enjoy the best of it.

Kaunas old town

# Land and People

Six centuries ago, during Lithuania's pagan days, the forests were considered sacred and worshipped. Today, the people of Lithuania still treasure their woodlands. The poet Sigitas Geda reflected this national passion when he wrote that 'a person who does not understand the earth, the ocean and the trees is a barbarian'.

Lakeside living in eastern Lithuania

Flanked by the Baltic Sea on the west, Lithuania shares its borders with four countries – Latvia, Belarus, Poland and Russia (the Kaliningrad region). It is located right in the middle of Europe – in fact, a spot 26km north of Vilnius (*see pp66–7*) has been designated as the centre of Europe by the French National Geographical Institute. Extending over 65,300sq km, Lithuania is approximately the same size as Ireland, twice the size of Belgium, and bigger than both Denmark and Switzerland. It is both the largest and, with 3.6 million inhabitants, the most densely populated of the Baltic states.

With over 90km of pale sands along the Baltic coast, constituting most of the country's western border, and a predominance of gentle rolling plains and extensive forests, the country's landscape is diverse. Amounting to 55 per cent of the total land area, the plains comprise three lowland regions – the Pajuris Lowland, the Middle Lowland and the Eastern Lowland – and three upland plateaus – the Žemaičiai or Baltic Upland, the Aukštaičiai Upland and the Eastern Upland. Juozapine Hill (293.6m), not far from the capital Vilnius, is the highest point in Lithuania. The soil of the Middle Lowland plains, especially near the rivers, is the most fertile.

Woodlands today constitute only about 28 per cent of the total land area of this once heavily forested country. The dominant species are pine, spruce and birch; ash and oak groves are now scarce. The forests are rich in mushrooms and berries too.

The country boasts a fairly large network of waterways. There are nearly 3,000 lakes which cover over 880sq m in all. The biggest concentration of bodies of water is in the eastern part of the country, although the largest inland body of water, the Kuršių Marios (Curonian Lagoon), is in the west, separating the Kuršių Nerija (Curonian Spit) from the mainland and the Baltic Sea (*see p88*).

**Geographical Data**

The populations of the main cities are as follows – Vilnius: 580,000; Kaunas: 414,000; Klaipėda: 203,000; Šiaulių:147,000.
The longest rivers – Nemunas: 937.4km; Neris: 509.5km; Venta: 346km.
The largest lakes – Drūkšiai: 4479ha; Dysnai: 2439.4ha; Dusia: 2334.2ha.
The highest hills – Juozapine: 293.6m; Nevaišių: 288.9m.

Lithuania's five national parks (*see p128*) reflect the ecological diversity of the different geographical terrains. Established over 20 years ago, the parks protect forested land in the southern part of the country, the lakes in the northeast and the seaboard in the west. All the parks include exhibits and collections of local cultural heritage, mostly to be found in their tourist information centres. As well as providing protection for the natural environment, the national parks of Lithuania are outstanding places for recreation and relaxation. Their popularity as destinations for active holidays is on the increase, and accommodation can be found in a range of traditional village houses and hostels as well as the occasional hotel.

**Ethnographic Regions**

Lithuania is broadly divided into four main regions, which are ethnographically and ecologically distinct. Aukštaitija, Dzūkija, Suvalkija and Žemaitija differ from each other in their character, dialects and folk traditions, and also their flora and fauna.

The largest region, Aukštaitija covers the middle, east and north of the country. The name is derived from the word *aukstai* meaning 'high', after the hilly uplands in this region. Aukštaitija is extremely popular with tourists in summer because of its fine forests and

## Lithuania

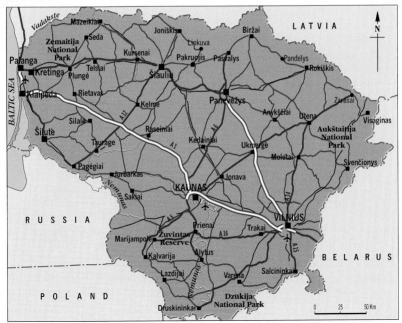

Evening shadows in a Klaipėda street

Suvalkija, in the southwest, is the smallest region and is named after the town of Suvalkų, which now lies across the border in Poland. The proximity to Poland may have a bearing on the region's culinary speciality, *skilandis*, which is a kind of smoked sausage filled with savoury minced meat. The region is mainly agricultural, with small land-holdings characterised by farmsteads surrounded by trees. In folklore, Suvalkijan farmers are known for their orderliness, pragmatism, efficiency – and a tendency towards miserliness.

Dzūkija, the southern region of Lithuania, borders Poland and Belarus. Flanking the River Nemunas, most of it is under forest cover. A major feature of the region therefore relates to woodland culture – carvings can be seen in plenty on the roadsides and in the forests themselves. Botanical reserves and ancient villages connected to the life of the forest reinforce this culture. In season, mushrooms on the forest floors draw pickers from far afield. With their legendary optimism, the Dzukijans are renowned for their love of song and zeal in the preservation of local tradition. The region's main town is the famous old health spa of Druskininkai, which attracts many Lithuanians and foreign tourists to this area.

Recorded as Samogitia as early as the 13th century, Žemaitija is the westernmost region of the country. The locals are an industrious lot, but not noted for a propensity to change. The Žemaitija National Park is very popular in summer, but the region's claim to fame is as the country's dairy centre. An interesting peculiarity of the region is

beautiful lakes. This area has the largest number of lakes, with the country's largest (Drūkšiai) and deepest (Tauragnas) ones both located here. The forests here are some of the oldest in the country and lay claim to the oldest tree, the 1,500-year-old oak tree in Stelmuzee.

In the settled countryside, farms tend to be divided into smaller holdings. Many in this area have been designated ethnographic farms, where the attempt is to maintain a traditional way of life. There are plenty of information centres and museums too, including the Beekeeping Museum in Stripeikiai (*see pp124–5*). For the beer enthusiast, two of Lithuania's largest breweries are also in this region – in Utena and Panevėžys.

the Zemaitukai horse. In danger of extinction until recently, this short, strong and energetic beast is happily beginning to increase in number.

## Climate

The climate of Lithuania is transitional between maritime and continental. The maritime climate prevails in the 12–15km-wide coastal zone in the west, while towards the eastern part, it becomes continental. Lithuania's climate in general is considered salubrious and favourable for economic activities.

The country is characterised by roughly four seasons, with moderate heat in summer. Summers are also marked by normal humidity as well as an adequate number of sunny days. Winters, however, are long, and the period of vegetative growth short (169–202 days). July is the warmest time of the year, with temperatures rising to the mid-twenties. Average precipitation in Lithuania has been recorded at 660mm per annum.

## Ethnic Groups

In contrast to the mixed populations of Lithuania's Baltic neighbours, over 80 per cent of the country's population is ethnic Lithuanian. However, there are people of an unbelievable 115 different ethnic backgrounds scattered throughout the country. The second largest ethnic group is Poles (6.9 per cent) who, unsurprisingly, mainly live in the southeast of the country. Other large groups are Russians (8.2 per cent), Belarusians (1.5 per cent), Ukrainians (1 per cent) and Jews (0.12 per cent).

Possibly as a result of the Lithuanian

The Holy Trinity Church in Vilnius

experience of occupation and oppression over the centuries, there is great respect shown to ethnic minorities and their rights are protected in the country's legislation. This respect for minorities is enshrined in the Constitution of the Republic of Lithuania, guaranteeing them the right to cultivate their own language, traditions and culture. The 1989 Law on Ethnic Minorities, amended in 1991, guarantees all citizens of the Republic of Lithuania, regardless of their ethnic background, equal political, social and economic rights, besides guaranteeing the cultural integrity of minorities; the law also encourages the expression of their national consciousness.

There is a special government department dedicated to the needs of minority communities. This department also looks after the needs of Lithuanians living abroad and is the first of its kind in Eastern and Central Europe. Bilingual education is promoted and Lithuanian radio and TV stations broadcast in a number of different languages. Publication of periodicals and newspapers in languages other than Lithuanian are encouraged, as are the establishment and membership of public organisations for ethnic minorities. Other European countries could learn a thing or two from Lithuania's policies for its ethnic minorities.

All the diversity that makes up the Lithuanian society today has by no means meant a diminution of indigenous culture and beliefs. The high percentage of ethnic Lithuanians has made it relatively easy for them to nurture and preserve their culture,

Typical Lithuanian woodcarvings

and their traditions remain as strong as ever.

### Religion

Before the acceptance of Christianity in 1387, pagan religious practices were the norm for Lithuanians and remained popular in folk culture for several hundred years afterwards.

In contemporary Lithuanian society, the dominant religion is Roman Catholic, professed by most Lithuanians and the ethnic Poles. According to population census data, over 70 per cent of all residents subscribe to the Catholic Church. Roman Catholicism appeared in the Grand Duchy of Lithuania in the 14th century, around the same time as the emergence of Karaite, Jewish and Tartar religious traditions in the country. Protestants made an appearance only in the 16th century and were joined by the Old Believers in the 17th century. The majority of those of Russian origin belong to the Russian Orthodox Church.

The Constitution does not make provision for a state religion but specifically protects the freedom of thought, conscience and religion of all Lithuanian citizens. The state recognises traditional Lithuanian churches and religious organisations as well as other denominations and religious organisations, provided that they have a commitment to Lithuanian society and their teachings and rituals do not contradict morality or the law. The 1995 Law on Religious Societies and Communities confirmed nine religious groups as recognised by the state: Roman Catholics, Greek Catholics (Uniates), the Orthodox Church, Old Believers, Evangelical Reformers, Evangelical Lutherans, Jews, Karaites and Sunni Muslims. These communities have coexisted in Lithuania for over 300 years. The 1995 Law also includes provisions for the procedures that religious communities need to follow in order to obtain

state recognition. The Seimas (Parliament) may award this recognition on the following conditions: the religious community needs to have been formally registered and to have been practising in the country for at least 25 years. The community also needs to have public support and must be adequately integrated into Lithuanian society and cultural heritage.

Catholic churches are a common sight in most Lithuanian towns

# History

| | |
|---|---|
| **7th–2nd centuries BC** | The first Baltic tribes establish themselves on the territory that is now known as Lithuania. |
| **AD 1009** | The first mention of Lithuania in written text, in the *Kvedlinburgh Chronicle*. |
| **1236** | The Battle of Saule. Duke Mindaugas defeats the Livonian Knights and unites local chieftains, establishing the state of Lithuania. |
| **1253** | Duke Mindaugas crowned Lithuania's king on July 6th, now celebrated as the day of Lithuanian statehood. |
| **1263** | Lithuania's first and only king, Mindaugas, is killed. |
| **1323** | First mention of Vilnius in written text during the reign of the Grand Duke Gediminas. The Grand Duke sent letters to various Western European towns inviting craftsmen and merchants to settle in the city. |
| **1325** | Gediminas forms an alliance with Poland by marrying his daughter to the Polish king's son. |
| **1387** | Lithuania converts to Christianity. |
| **1390** | Vilnius, its buildings mostly of timber, is burnt by Teutonic knights. |
| **1392–1430** | Reign of Vytautas the Great. |
| **1410** | The Battle of Žalgiris (Grunwals): joint Lithuanian–Polish forces defeat the Teutonic Order. |
| **1430** | Lithuanian borders are extended from the Baltic coast to the Black Sea. |
| **1569** | The Lublin Union: a Polish–Lithuanian state is established. |
| **16th century** | The Renaissance Era: the golden era of Vilnius and Lithuania as a whole. |
| **1579** | The founding of Vilnius University. |
| **1795** | Lithuania is annexed by the Tsar. Vilnius becomes the centre of a province, and its walls are destroyed. |
| **1831** | Amidst significant revolt against the Tsar, Vilnius University is shut down and Catholic churches |

| | | | |
|---|---|---|---|
| | closed and converted to Russian Orthodox use. | **1940** | The Soviet Union occupies and annexes the Republic of Lithuania. |
| **1834** | Installation of an optical telegraph line, stretching from St Petersburg to Vilnius to Warsaw. | **1941–44** | Lithuania is occupied by Germany. |
| **1861** | Serfdom abolished. | **1990** | The Supreme Council of the Republic of Lithuania declares the restoration of independence. |
| **1863** | Another revolt against the Tsar fails and oppressive measures are increased. | **1991** | Lithuania joins the United Nations. |
| **1905** | Russia is defeated by Japan, signalling the decline of the Tsarist empire. | **1993** | Soviet troops are finally withdrawn. |
| **1918** | The Council of Lithuania proclaims the restoration of an independent Lithuanian state on 16th February. | **1994** | Lithuania joins the NATO Partnership for Peace Programme. Signs treaty of friendship with Poland. |
| **1920** | Poland gains control of Vilnius. Kaunas becomes the Lithuanian capital. | **2003** | Rolandas Paksas is elected President in January. Lithuanian voters (90 per cent) say yes to EU accession. |
| **1939** | The secret signing of the Molotov–Ribbentrop pact between Stalin and Hitler, dividing up Europe between the two states. This puts Lithuania back under Soviet influence. Later in the year, the Soviets restore Vilnius as its capital, under the Soviet–Lithuanian agreement, in return for the right to set up military bases there. | **2004** | Lithuania becomes a member of both the EU and NATO. |
| | | **2005** | A Russian fighter crashes on Lithuanian territory. Diplomatic tension with Moscow increases. The situation is defused when investigations find technical and human error to blame. |

# From Occupation to Independence

Lithuania's difficult fate through the 20th century can be largely attributed to the Molotov–Ribbentrop pact (*see box*), which contained a secret appendix. This was an agreement on how the then independent countries of Europe would be divided between the two totalitarian regimes of Germany and the USSR. The countries included in the pact were Estonia, Latvia, Lithuania, Poland and Romania. Originally Soviet control was to cover only Latvia, Estonia and Finland, but Lithuania was later included in the package as well. Poland was to be partitioned between the two. All these countries were invaded by either the Soviets or Nazi Germany, or both at some point during the Second World War.

Once the partition of Poland was complete, the Soviets wasted no time in exerting huge pressure on the countries in their sphere of influence. The USSR wanted to place a number of bases in all these countries and make several adjustments to their territories. They persevered until all the states, except Finland, had signed pacts of 'defence

and mutual assistance', which allowed the USSR to set up Soviet bases in their countries. Lithuania was invaded and annexed by the USSR in 1940, and then occupied by Germany from 1941 to 1944, when it was retaken by the Soviets. These two occupations led to the near disappearance of the Jewish community under Hitler's 'final solution'; at the same time, tens of thousands of Lithuanians were deported to Siberia. The devastation and suffering experienced by these deportations is vividly recorded in an excellent exhibition in the Genocide Victims Museum in Vilnius (*see pp41–3*).

The Soviets imposed a totalitarian system on Lithuania, which included a planned economy, one-party rule, surveillance and terror carried out by the NKVD and later the KGB.

## MOLOTOV–RIBBENTROP PACT

Officially known as the Treaty of Nonaggression between Germany and the Union of Soviet Socialist Republic, this Nazi–Soviet Pact in theory was one of non-aggression between the Soviet Union and the German Third Reich. It was signed on the 23rd of August 1939, by the two respective foreign ministers, Vyacheslav Molotov (Soviet Union) and Joachim Ribbentrop (Germany), which led to it being known as the Molotov-Ribbentrop pact. This non-aggression lasted just short of two years, broken in June 1941 by German invasion of the Soviet Union.

At the end of the Second World War, resistance against the Soviets remained pretty strong in Lithuania. The Khrushchev era, which followed the death of Stalin, brought about a slight liberalisation though. Lithuanians gradually began to make inroads into the Communist Party.

In 1988, the founding of the Sajūdis movement marked a turning point in Lithuanian history. The Sajūdis, along with like-minded Estonian and Latvian groups, celebrated the 50th anniversary of the Molotov–Ribbentrop Pact in 1989 by organising the largest-ever mass protest in the Baltic states: over two million people linked hands in a human chain that covered a distance of 650km all the way from Tallinn in Estonia to Vilnius in Lithuania.

Finally, in February 1990, after over 50 years of Soviet occupation, Sajūdis won a sweeping majority of the seats in the local Supreme Council elections, and in March 1990 Lithuania was able to proclaim its independence, the first of the Soviet-occupied states to do so. However, Moscow refused to accept this. Its attempts at resisting change and forced intervention led to 14 unarmed civilians being killed at the TV tower in Vilnius.

In 1991, Moscow finally recognised Lithuanian independence. Later that year, Lithuania attained international recognition when it was admitted to the United Nations on September 17th. The Lithuanian currency, the litas, was reintroduced in 1993; in February of the same year, Algirdas Brazauskas became the first directly elected President of Lithuania.

Also in 1993, the last Soviet troops left Lithuania. The country voted to join the EU in 2003 and was granted membership in May 2004. Later in the same year, it became a member of NATO, becoming an independent player in the global scenario.

Facing page: Grim reminders of Lithuania's constant struggle against invading powers

## HUMAN TRAGEDIES IN LITHUANIA IN THE MID-20TH CENTURY

| | |
|---|---|
| 1941: (first 6 months) | Repatriation of Lithuania's Germans (50,000 people); the first mass deportations to the Soviet Union (23,000) |
| 1941–44 | Nazi genocide of the Jews (220,000 people) |
| 1943–44 | 10,000 people taken to forced labour in Germany; 60,000 flee to the West |
| 1945 | 140,000 inhabitants of the Klaipėda district emigrate |
| 1945–46 | 200,000 Poles deported ('repatriated') to Poland |
| 1941–51 | About 25,000 resistance fighters and 10,000 Soviet activists and supporters killed |
| 1945–53 | Mass deportations to Siberia and other eastern parts of the Soviet Union (250,000) |

# Governance

Lietuvos Respubliką (The Republic of Lithuania) is now a stable state that is governed by a system of parliamentary democracy. Formally known as the Lithuanian Soviet Socialist Republic, Lithuania declared independence from the Soviet Union in March 1990 although the Soviet Union did not recognise Lithuania's independence until the 6th of September 1991.

The Lithuanian flag: yellow stands for the sun, the green for nature and the red for blood

The foundations of the political and social system are enforced by the Fundamental Law (the Constitution) which was adopted on the 25th of October 1992. The Constitution also sets out the rights, freedoms and obligations of citizens. The powers of the state are shared between the Seimas (Parliament), the President, the Government and the Judiciary. The scope of the

powers of each of these branches is defined by the Constitution.

## Seimas (Parliament)

The supreme body of state power in Lithuania is the Seimas. At present it comprises 141 deputies, who are elected for a four-year period. Of the 141 seats in the Seimas, 71 members are directly elected by popular vote while the remaining 70 are elected by proportional representation. The Seimas has a wide range of powers, consisting of the following:

• The power to adapt and amend the Constitution.

• The power to adopt laws, to consider drafts on the programmes produced by the Government and to approve them.

• The power to control the activities of the Government, to approve the budget of the Government, and to

Seimas, the Parliament building in Vilnius

**Lithuania's Political Parties**
Action of Lithuanian Poles
Homeland Union/Conservative Party
The Labour Party
The Liberal and Centre Union
The Liberal Democratic Party
The Lithuanian Christian Democrats or LKD
The Lithuanian People's Union for a Fair Lithuania
The Lithuanian Social Democratic Coalition, which consists of the Lithuanian Democratic Labour Party or LDDP and the Lithuanian Social Democratic Party or LSDP
The New Democracy and Farmers' Union
The Social Liberals (New Union)
The Social Union of Christian Conservatives
The Young Lithuania and New Nationalists.

**Administrative Divisions**
The country's ten administrative divisions are as follows: Alytaus, Kauno, Klaipėdos, Marijampolės, Panevėžio, Šiaulių, Tauragės, Telšių, Utenos and Vilniaus. Each administrative unit is entitled to the right of self-government, which is implemented through Local Government Councils. Lithuanian citizens and other permanent residents of an administrative unit can be elected according to the law to Local Government Councils for a four-year term on the basis of universal, equal and direct suffrage. Voting is by secret ballot by the citizens of Lithuania and other residents of that administrative unit. The procedure for the organisation and activities of self-government institutions is established by law. Local Government Councils form executive bodies, which are accountable to the Councils for the direct implementation of the laws of the Republic of Lithuania and the decisions of the Government and the Local Government Council (Constitution of the Republic of Lithuania, Article 119).

The newly cleaned pillars of the Rotušės (Town Hall) in Vilnius

establish the state institutions provided by the law.

• The power to appoint and to dismiss chairpersons of the state institutions, and to settle other issues pertaining to state power.

### The President

The highest official of the state, the President of Lithuania is elected for a five-year term directly by the Lithuanian citizens on the basis of universal, equal and direct suffrage by secret ballot (citizens must be over 18 to vote). The President plays a key role through the following functions:

• To consider major political problems of foreign and home affairs.

• To appoint and dismiss state officials as provided by the Constitution and other laws.

• To proclaim a state of emergency if required.

• To approve and publish the laws adopted by the Seimas or return them with remarks for reconsideration.

• To perform other duties as specified in the Constitution.

**Lithuanian Membership of International Organisations**

The Republic of Lithuania is a member of many international organisations, the most significant of these being the European Union, the United Nations, NATO and the World Trade Organisation.

In June 2004, Valdas Adamkus was elected President of the Republic of Lithuania. The next election is to be held in June 2009.

## The Government

The Lithuanian Government comprises the Prime Minister and Ministers. The Prime Minister is appointed or dismissed by the President, with the approval of the Seimas. Ministers are also appointed and dismissed by the President, based on the recommendation of the Prime Minister. Within the limits of its competence, the Government's duties are as follows:

• To control the affairs of the country.
• To guard the inviolability of the territory, that is, the Republic.
• To ensure state and civilian security.
• To carry out resolutions of the Seimas on the enforcement of laws and the decrees of the President.
• To enter into diplomatic relations with foreign countries and international organisations, and to maintain them.
• To perform the duties specified in the Constitution and other laws.

## The Judiciary

The Lithuanian legal system is based on the civil law system, in which all legislative acts can be appealed to the courts. This judicial system was established by Article 9 of the Constitution, and the Law on Courts passed in 1994. The judiciary has three branches: the Constitutional Court, the Supreme Court and the Court of Appeal. The judges for all courts are appointed by the President.

## Citizens' Rights

All Lithuanian citizens have the right to participate in the government, both directly and through their freely elected representatives. They have the right of equal opportunity to serve in a state office. Each citizen is guaranteed the right to criticise the work of state institutions and their officers, and to appeal against their decisions. It is prohibited to persecute citizens for expressing this criticism. Citizens are also guaranteed the right to petition.

One of the many commemorative statues to national heroes

# Culture

As a nation, Lithuanians are extremely proud of their culture and traditions. Through the many years of oppressive Soviet occupation, Lithuania succeeded in holding on to its culture and character, its art, music, song and dance. Today, classical music traditions thrive side by side with vibrant folk ones. These elements of culture combine to provide an enriching experience for visitors.

Vilnius Art Gallery – spanning four centuries

### Folk Music

Much Lithuanian folklore is based upon a rural outlook on life, with songs as an integral and popular part of folk tradition. Folk music is at the heart of the Lithuanian cultural heritage – its folk songs must number over half a million. There are songs for every occasion, and most date from feudal times. Lithuanian folk songs are divided into categories such as family songs, historical and war songs, songs of protest, songs of Lithuanian emigrants, and many others. Elegiac songs are central to Lithuanian folklore.

There are many work songs which used to accompany all kinds of field and household chores: haymaking, harvesting, processing of flax, grinding grain, spinning, weaving and many other rural activities. Social contradictions too are expressed in work songs, orphan songs and songs about the hard lot of women. War and historical songs tend to be less specific, not necessarily mentioning concrete historical facts or indicating particular towns, villages or rivers. They usually feature images of seeing off a soldier to war and the period of waiting for his return. An important figure in these war songs is the soldier's personified steed: the horse is his messenger and the song is usually about the bond between the soldier and his family.

### Song and Dance Festival
The immensely popular Song and Dance Celebration that occurs every four years in Lithuania has received international recognition, with UNESCO listing it as one of the Masterpieces of Oral and Intangible Heritage of Humanity. Festivals of this kind taking place in the neighbouring Baltic states are also on this list. The next festival in Lithuania is to be held in 2007.

Detail of bas relief sculpture in Kaunas

## Folk Choreography

Lithuanians, like their neighbours in the other Baltic states, have always loved to dance. Young people gather in the fields to dance during the summer months, and in farmhouses in winter. Older people and small children also take part in these festivities, talking, socialising and generally amusing themselves. Dance is central to Lithuanian folk traditions. Lithuanian folk choreography can be classified into four groups: polyphonic singing dances, ring or circle dances, games and other dances.

These creative dances involve artistic imagery created by rhythmical movements to vocal or instrumental music. Folk choreography, like other branches of folk art, is an expression of the nation's customs, way of life and work. The life of the Lithuanian nation, its character and principles are reflected in the content of Lithuanian dance. Every movement and step in the dance has a purpose. The dance movements are intended to be a visible expression of emotion. Even a slight change of movement can symbolise a change in mood. The originality of the dance and the methods of expression used in the choreography are influenced by the creator's situation at that time. They are an expression of their racial characteristics, geographic surroundings and the relationship of Lithuania with the surrounding nations. By creating a dance, Lithuanians simultaneously create a story.

The form of the dance depends on whether it has been created by a man or a woman. In this agricultural country, creation of folk art was mainly a female

Dancers in traditional Lithuanian dress

activity, and therefore often related to feminine themes (for example, the work done by women only). This of course also influenced the expression of choreography – for example, the long skirts worn by women result in simplicity in the steps.

The distinctiveness of Lithuanian folk choreography is also displayed in the music used. The rhythm is calm and balanced, and the tempo is moderate. It is also purely lyrical, and tends to be narrative. Interestingly, in the war songs, the actual battle is never described. Unfortunately there are no war dances left. Hunting dances have not survived either.

The first reference to the art of the Baltic Movement was at the end of the 9th century, by the traveller Vulfstan. Other travellers' accounts also mention how the Prussians and Lithuanians played and danced. Until the 20th century, dances were only occasionally documented and therefore only fragments of some dance descriptions can be found. Often only the name of the dance and its mood were recorded. All the dances during this period were recorded orally; the music, steps or movements are not described. From these recordings one can only reconstruct the character of the dance for the most part.

From around the middle of the 20th century, two completely separate genres of folk dance movement have developed in Lithuania. The new type that has emerged is a stylised one, created by professional choreographers using music specially written by a professional composer.

However, the genre of the traditional folk dance is still alive. Younger people learn these dances from their parents or grandparents, whose lives have been greatly influenced by customs and traditions, and who have mastered the art of these folk dances that they learned directly from their parents at outdoor country parties. The dances are also kept alive by folk groups, which still participate in folklore collection outings in the rural areas.

## Literature

Most literary traditions begin with religious writings, and Lithuania is no exception. The country's literary tradition is considered to have begun with the appearance of Martynas Mažvydas' *Catechismus* in 1547. Lithuanian fiction did not really feature as an art form until the 19th

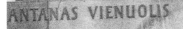

Statue in Anykščiai of the distinguished writer Antanas Zukauskas who wrote under the pseudonym Vienuolis

Well-known political poet, Adam Mickiewicz who wrote *Pan Taduesz*, Poland's national epic

century, linking in with the general era of national reawakening. A famous early literary figure of the country was Kristijonas Donelaitis (1714–1780). His poem *The Seasons* was published in 1818, over half a century after it was written. Translated into many languages, it is now considered a national epic.

The end of the 18th to the beginning of the 20th century was a difficult period for Lithuanian literature under the rule of the Russian Empire, and only a few exceptional poets emerged. Antanas Baranauskas and Maironis were two such, and they managed to elicit some protection from the secular authorities because of their status in the church. Much of the great flowering of literature at the beginning of the 20th century can be seen as an attempt to rouse people to struggle for independence. Some of the great names of this period are Zemaite, the founder of realist prose; the master of the

psychological novel, Jonas Biliūnas, two patriotic writers Vincas Krėvė and Juozas Tumas-Vaizgantas, and poet, prose writer and playwright Balys Sruoga. The memoirs of the last, about his experiences in a concentration camp, are one of the few works of that time published in English, under the title *Forest of the Gods*. A large number of Lithuania's finest writers of the 20th century fled the country during the Second World War, while some suffered grim periods of incarceration and torture, often ending in death. Interestingly, 70 per cent of the members of the Lithuanian Writers Union chose exile rather than live under Stalin. It was only after independence in 1990 that the previously banned works of partisans and deportees were published. Miškinis's *Broken Crosses* and Kazys Inčiūra's *The Psalms of Captivity* are two examples.

Looking at Lithuanian literature as a whole, the period of the 1940s and 1950s was devastating. It is only in the last few years that some of the émigré writers have been returning to Lithuania. A significant example is Czeslaw Milosz, who won the Nobel Prize for Literature in 1980. Born in Lithuania in 1911, Milosz lived away from the country from 1951 but died in his native land in 2004. Poetry was his main domain, but one of his two novels, *The Issa Valley*, is set in rural Lithuania. He also wrote some political non-fiction works of which *Captive Mind* is worth reading. Those wishing to sample excerpts from current and classical Lithuanian literature should consult the *Vilnius*, the magazine of the Lithuanian Writers Union.

## Art

From early times up to about the 13th and 14th centuries, art in Lithuania mainly consisted of decorative carving in wood. However, after the arrival of Christianity, Lithuanian fine arts tended to develop along religious lines. Portraits of senior clergy and the nobility became popular, as did illustrated manuscripts and biblical scenes. To appreciate the development of art in Lithuania to the end of the 19th century, visit Vilnius's Chodkevicius Palace, which has an excellent collection of paintings covering this period.

Detail of a sculpture in Kaunas' main square

The setting up of the Architecture Department at Vilnius University in 1793 marked the establishment of professional fine arts in Lithuania. It was led by the first exponent of Classicism, Laurynas Stuoka-Gucevicius. Pranciškus Smuglevičius was the first Professor of the Department of Drawing and Painting when it was set up in 1797. It was due to Smuglevicius's reputation that the Vilnius Arts School became a leading artistic centre in Lithuania and Poland. The department was later

headed by the famous portrait painter Jonas Rustemas, and his teaching in the early 19th century had a huge influence on the development of Lithuanian painting.

Another landmark on the arts scene was the establishment of the Lithuanian Arts Society at the beginning of the century. The first exhibition of professional and folk art was mounted in 1914. The combination of professional and folk art became a feature of the Lithuanian art scene, taking on a deep cultural importance.

In 1920, the Lithuanian Society of Artists was founded in Kaunas. Another significant event during this time was the opening of the Ciurlionis Art Gallery in 1925, also in Kaunas. This gallery housed both the works of the great man and a collection of other professional and folk art.

The modern era in Lithuanian art dates from 1950 and thrived under the relative liberalisation of the Krushchev regime. Graphic art in the 1950s and 60s was mainly concerned with interpretations of folk art. Petras Repsys (b. 1940) is one of the outstanding figures in contemporary graphic art. His frescoes can be seen at Vilnius University and have come to be known as a significant expression of Baltic culture, incorporating historical, mythological and day-to-day aspects of tradition.

The last decade of the 20th century has seen a huge change in artistic expression. Art institutions have changed dramatically, and state-owned galleries and private galleries have appeared alongside each other. Two new arts centres opened in the 1990s, and have inspired new trends and forms of artistic language – the Vilnius Contemporary Arts Centre and the Soros Contemporary Arts Centre.

Other traditions that are still very strong include various types of handicraft. Around the country in many of the national parks are scattered numerous examples of woodcarvings. Handcrafted articles of wood, amber and linen make great souvenirs.

### Theatre and Music

The Tsarist regime banned theatre in the 19th century, but the Lithuanians kept it alive by running secret performances in barns or village houses. After 1904, when the Tsarist regime was forced to repeal its prohibition of the Latin alphabet, cultural societies began to appear all around the country. These societies encouraged the development of choirs, dance groups and drama societies, and helped to develop a national consciousness in theatre and other performances. The Society founded in Kaunas embraced all cultural forms and engendered the first cultural institutions: the Art School, the Conservatoire and the State Theatre.

The period of Soviet occupation was a stultifying time for the national theatre. Today, however, Lithuanian theatre has no shortage of talented directors and is thriving once more.

The Second World War and the Soviet occupation also took its toll on the development of Lithuanian music. Mikalojus Ciurlionis (*see p24*) is considered the founder of modern Lithuanian music and some of his compositions are typical of early 20th-century European music. A radical and innovative group of composers then emerged to challenge the musical scene, but the establishment of Soviet rule resulted in a return to the highly traditional, 19th-century Romantic style. This was to change in the 1980s when the new Romantics appeared with their literary and neo-Romantic ideas, espousing the cause of the minimalist styles that are a feature of folk music and trying to emulate their simplicity of rhythm and melody (*see Directory p146*).

The MK Ciurlionis State Art Museum

# Festivals and Events

## January

### Epiphany, Vilnius

The three Biblical kings walk the streets of the city, blessing children and giving them presents.

### The Lake Sartai Horse Races

Horse races take place on the frozen Lake Sartai, which is near Utena; they are also sometimes held in Duestos city. The first races occur in January, when the riders must qualify for the national races held on the first Saturday in February.

## February

### Lithuanian Independence Day

A national holiday to mark Lithuania's independence, 16 February is celebrated in all parts of the country. Each area celebrates the restoration of the Lithuanian state in different ways.

### The Vilnius Book Fair

This professional cultural forum is the biggest annual fair of its kind in the Baltic states, attended by over 50,000 people. It is organised by the Lithuanian Publishers' Association each February. *www.bookfair@litexp.lt*

### Shrove Tuesday

This day marks the end of winter and the beginning of Lent. The date is variable, depending on Easter, and may occur in March in some years. Observed all over the country, it is celebrated in a particularly entertaining fashion in Vilnius. Various events, such as the burning of a symbol of winter on Tauras Hill, symbolise the driving away of winter. All day the streets of Vilnius are full of people in different costumes. *www.vilnius.lt*

## March

### The Kaziukas Street Fair, Vilnius

Held on the first weekend of March, this is a traditional folk arts and crafts fair dedicated to the Patron Saint of Lithuania, St Casimir. Events take place across the whole city.

### The Spring Equinox

The Flag of Earth is hoisted and people plant trees to mark the Spring Equinox in Lithuania. (20–21 March)

## April

### International Jazz Festival, Kaunas

This is one of the most popular jazz festivals in Europe, featuring top international acts.

### The International Dance Festival, Vilnius

One of the most outstanding festivals in the Baltic states, this is a celebration of the New Baltic Dance.

## May

### International Folklore Festival (Skamba, Skamba Kankliai), Vilnius

This end-of-May festival attracts folk performers from all over Lithuania as well as from other countries. Concerts are held in the streets of the Old Town.

## June

### Vilnius Festival

Since 1997, the Vilnius Festival has been held every summer. It starts in June and continues till July, featuring internationally renowned performers in the world of classical music. Both traditional and modern music are presented. Each year the festival embraces a different theme. The venues include the National Opera and Ballet Theatre, the Great Courtyard of Vilnius University and St Bernardine's Church.

**The Feast of St John's Night (Joninės)**
This mystical event marks the summer solstice. Bonfires are lit, songs sung and pagan rituals revisited.

## July
**The Annual Festival of Country Music, Visaginas**
Held in the 30-year-old Russian-speaking town of Visaginas, this is one of the smallest of its kind in the world.

## August
**St Christopher Summer Music Festival, Vilnius**
Festival of jazz, classical, organ and pop music.

## September
**International Festival, Vilnius**
Festival demonstrating Lithuania's place in the world of jazz. It is the oldest annual event held in Vilnius.

**International Fire Sculpture Festival, Vilnius**
Held on the Autumn Equinox.

**Grok Jurgeli, Kaunas**
This is a festival of folk music.

**Autumn Equinox (Gediminas Day)**
Occurring at the end of September, this marks the end of the earth's fertility. Plays based on old traditions and customs are performed throughout the country.

## November
**All Souls Day**
Candles are lit at cemeteries across the country on 2nd November.

## December
**Blukas Holiday**
This holiday marks the shortest day of the year, 23rd December. Old logs, symbolising evil spirits, are dragged down the streets and burnt. A nativity play is held in Vilnius.

International Folklore Festival, Vilnius

Western markets. However, since Lithuania conducts much more trade with Russia, more than the other two Baltic States, it was significantly affected by the 1998 Russian financial crisis, from which it is finally recovering. Lithuania's gradual economic recovery has been facilitated by a combination of international and domestic factors, rising domestic consumption and growing investment. Privatisation of the large, state-owned utilities, particularly in the energy sector, is nearing completion. Overall, more than 80 per cent of enterprises have been privatised. This is a giant leap towards a modern market economy from the central planning installed by the Soviets.

Ⓞne of the fastest growing economies of the European Union, the Lithuanian economy has greatly benefitted from the country's geographical position. Its location facilitates trade with both Eastern and

Of the three Baltic States, Lithuania's economy is the largest and overall it is the most diverse. The industrial sector, in particular, is extremely varied, and includes the production of chemicals, electronics, household appliances, pharmaceuticals, wood and wood processing and the food industry.

Trade is now increasingly oriented towards the Western market. Lithuania's membership of the World Trade Organisation and

the European Union since 2004 has also aided its economic growth. Its strategic position is also attractive to foreign investors who seek to attract business from the countries of the Baltic rim. Foreign government and business support have helped in the transition from the old command economy to a market economy. As a result of these factors, the unemployment rate dropped from 11 per cent in 2003 to 8 per cent in 2004.

However, the picture is not entirely rosy – many Lithuanians still struggle to make ends meet.

## The European Union and Tourism

Lithuania was one of the 10 countries granted accession to the European Union in 2004. Membership of the EU has undoubtedly contributed to Lithuania's impressive economic growth in the last few years. As it surges forward economically, Lithuanians speak of a 'Baltic tiger' similar to the 'Celtic tiger' tag used to describe Ireland. This economic development has undeniably been aided by membership of the European Union.

The country's tourist infrastructure, which has always been quite strong, has been expanding with additional EU funding. Roads are of a high quality, especially the main motorways. Indeed, of the three Baltic states, Lithuania definitely has the best roads. The tourist industry is becoming very competitive:

new businesses, hotels, resorts, restaurants, ATMs, petrol stations and supermarkets are appearing rapidly in towns and cities across Lithuania. The relatively competitive pricing is highly attractive for travellers from other European countries, who have to contend with much higher prices at home for similar standards of service and facilites. No wonder Lithuania's tourism industry is booming.

Facing page above: A local woman working in the fields in eastern Lithuania; below: A quick and painless route to the Museum of the Higher Castle
This page below: An unusual modern fountain sets the scene in Vokiečių gatvė, Vilnius

# Impressions

One of Lithuania's biggest assets is its excellent location. Positioned precisely at the centre of Europe, it is one of the main crossroads of the continent. The west–east connection between Paris, Berlin and Moscow is via Lithuania's capital, Vilnius. The north–south line linking Helsinki with Athens also crosses the centre of Lithuania. Direct connections to most other European cities makes Vilnius, and hence Lithuania, an easily accessible destination.

Lithuania has dense forests and lush hillsides

Enjoying the summer sun

## When to Go

Although summer is the favoured time to visit Lithuania, the wide range of activities and sights make the country a delightful destination at any time of the year. This enchanting country offers places to see and things to do to suit all tastes and appetites for adventure year-round. Visiting Lithuania just before or after the peak season is a good idea, although the temperatures may be on the low side. If you travel at these times, not only do you avoid the crowds but you also have the pick of the best restaurants and hotels. If you decide to go during the summer months, booking in advance is highly recommended. But whenever you decide to visit this country dotted with beautiful castles, palaces and churches that tell stories of medieval times, you won't be disappointed.

## Spring

Just before the summer months, the temperatures start to rise and the days become longer. This time of year is great for visiting the many national parks that Lithuania has to offer for a glimpse of nature at its best (*see Getting Away pp128–39*). The cooler temperatures, as compared to summer, also make sightseeing in the cities more pleasurable.

### Summer

The Baltic coast is the place to be in the summer, with Palanga (*see pp94–7*) being the most popular summer resort. Its fabulous unspoilt beaches are a great place to relax. Cool down after a spell of hot sun with a dip in the Baltic Sea. Another wonderful summer destination is the Curonian Spit, which is a long spit of land between the Baltic Sea and the Curonian Lagoon. It offers unspoilt beaches, high dunes and scenic forest land. Lithuania's national parks and nature reserves are a must-visit in summer. You can simply relax by a lake, go boating or fishing, or indulge in spa treatment.

### Autumn

Early September marks the end of the tourist season. However, the weather can remain warm for a few weeks after this, and this period is known in Lithuania as 'Grandma's summer'. September is recommended for those travellers who are looking for more than relaxation on a beach. The cooler weather makes it more comfortable for sightseeing and

Typical Lithuanian house

Eclectic collection of farm buildings in Dzūkija

active adventure. Furthermore, the streets of the old towns are less packed and the churches and museums less crowded. The national parks and nature reserves are beautiful in autumn as the leaves start to change colour and fall to carpet the ground. The downside of travelling at this time of year is that tourist services and facilities tend to get curtailed and service hours shortened. The weather is also less dependable.

**Winter**
What better way to beat the winter blues than booking yourself into one of the spa treatment resorts here for a few days' pampering (*see pp74–5*). Palanga is peaceful at this time of year, a lovely place to visit at low season for a quiet rest. Many of its large number of spa hotels and sanatoriums stay open year round. In southern Lithuania, Druskininkai is the premier spa location. It is not a coastal resort, but has the charm of a stately town surrounded by forests. Lithuania is significantly colder at this time of year,

and you are more than likely to be surrounded by a frosty, snowy landscape. Depending on your mindset and tolerance for the cold, this can be a bonus – and the snow-covered vistas have their own magical charm. There is some skiing, but the flatness of the land in most areas is more suited for cross-country skiing rather than downhill runs.

**Where to Go**
The main cities make good weekend city-break destinations at any time of year with direct flights from most European cities available now (*see pp175–6*). Vilnius, the capital and largest city in Lithuania, is in the southeast of the country, on the River Neris, and has much to offer. It has an Old Town packed with history and interesting buildings, and its 'New Town' offers as much as any other European city, with many high-street shopping chains, a bustling café culture and exclusive restaurants. Vilnius's nightlife does not go off-peak either. The cities of Kaunas and Klaipėda are also busy year round.

The country's five main national parks, containing magnificent lakes and forests are a must-see for all visitors. These are the Aukštaitija, Dzūkija, Kuršių Nerija, Trakai Historic and Žemaitija national parks. There are many other regional parks and nature reserves as well.

Offering a combination of city and beach life, the Baltic coast is one of Lithuania's main attractions. One of the coast's attractions during the summer months is the contrast between the heat of the sun and the refreshing cool of the water.

Kaunas's oldest building, the castle, set at the meeting of the Neris and Nemunas rivers

## What to Wear

Layering is the key to comfort at all times of the year. July is the warmest month and January the coolest (*see p9 & p177*). In the summer it can get hot, so light, breathable clothes are advisable when sightseeing. However, the evenings may get a bit cold even in summer, so carry a light jacket. Bring a hat, gloves and scarf in winter, along with a heavy coat. Layers are particularly useful in winter; while it may be cold outside and you need to wrap up, if you stop at a café for a coffee, you will be blasted with heat inside. The same goes for restaurants and bars. It may not be very cold in spring and autumn, but the winds can be chilly; so bring a windcheater-style jacket if you're visiting at this time of year.

With the average precipitation being 660mm per annum, it will almost definitely rain at some point during your visit to Lithuania, therefore a light rain jacket and umbrella are essential. In winter, sturdy waterproof walking shoes are recommended.

## How to Get Around

There is a high standard of organised tours that run from the main cities to nearby sights. Information on timings and destinations are available from local tourist offices.

Taking public transport in the main cities and towns will not be your most enjoyable experience in Lithuania, especially during rush hour in Vilnius. However, private buses and trolleys provide a cheap alternative. Tickets for buses and trolley buses in Vilnius can be purchased at most newspaper kiosks.

Discreet little hideaway on the edge of the forest

Public transport is of high standard. (*See practical guide for information on buses, trains and ferries in each region pp186–8*). Comprehensive, up-to-date arrival and departure times of all Baltic ferries, planes, trains and buses are available on the *City Paper's* website: *www.BalticsWorldwide.com*

## Driving

Lithuanian roads were the pride and joy of the Soviets, and are still of a high standard today. The main motorway, A1, running from Vilnius to Klaipėda via Kaunas, is excellent.

Driving is on the right-hand side of the road, and passing is on the left. Traffic can be chaotic though, to put it mildly, so be careful if you decide to rent a car in Lithuania. While you may be a safe and experienced driver, the style and habits of Lithuanian drivers are somewhat less predictable. Seat belts are compulsory under law, but you may not find many Lithuanians themselves wearing them. Signposting throughout the country is generally good (*see also practical guide pp178–80*).

## Attitudes and Etiquette

Lithuanians are generally an outgoing, friendly and welcoming people. Lithuania is considered the most courageous of the Baltic states as demonstrated in their resistance to Soviet oppression. They are also known for being more emotional than their Baltic neighbours, and this can have an up side and a down side. While they are good-humoured, cheerful to the point of boisterous, and generally more talkative than their northern neighbours, they are also known to be hot-headed and more likely to get openly irritated if something does not sit right.

Most Lithuanians are pleased with the influx of tourists that has coincided with their EU membership. These hospitable folk will often go out of their way to try and help you. However, as a result of occasional mutual language difficulties, you may not always receive what you requested!

There aren't too many formalities that are required of visitors. However, out of general respect for local traditions and mores, it is always better to ask if you are in doubt as to whether something is acceptable or not.

Nude sunbathing is generally not encouraged. There is an area on the Curonian Spit that is designated 'naturist', but even that is divided into male and female zones.

When visiting some churches and

Tourists on Palanga beach

religious sights, it is sometimes required to cover the thighs and shoulders, so it is worth wearing or carrying longer garments.

## The Language

The official language is Lithuanian, but Russian, Polish and German are also spoken in some parts of the country. Those who lived through the occupations of Germany and Russia would be more likely to understand those languages, even if they may be reluctant to acknowledge it. Most people under 30 speak some English and will attempt to communicate in English if they hear you speaking English.

It is the oldest of the living languages of the Baltic States, dating back to the 5th century AD. It belongs to the family of Indo-European languages. Lithuanian is rich in dialects and regional accents

Enjoy a ride at the open-air Museum, Rumšiškės

and is spoken by some three million people in Lithuania, and by about a million people living in other countries such as Australia, Brazil, Belarus, Canada, Latvia, Poland, Russia and the USA.

Lithuanian is pretty much a phonetic language, which is an advantage for the traveller. When attempting to order in Lithuanian straight from a phrase book, sound out each letter, with the stress nearly always on the first syllable.

## Suggested Itineraries
### Seven-day trip to Lithuania
**Day 1:** Arrive in Vilnius in the morning. After checking into your hotel, explore the Old Town (listed on the UNESCO heritage list). This is one of the most beautiful old cities in Eastern Europe (*see walk p54*). Stay the night at Vilnius (*see accommodation listings pp170–71*).
**Day 2:** In the morning see other important sights that were not on the walk route, such as St Peter and St Paul Church and St Anne's Church. Or take the Circular Walk (*see p52*). In the afternoon, take a tour bus to Trakai. There are full-day and half-day trips on offer.
**Day 3:** Leave in the morning for Kaunas via Druskininkai. From there, follow the drive described on *p78*. You arrive at Kaunas in the afternoon. This is the second largest city in Lithuania and was

Traditional food to be washed down with an exotic wine

the capital between the two World Wars. It also boasts a fabulous Old Town (*see Walk p86*). If you have time, a trip to the Rumšiškės Open-Air Museum is recommended. (*see p60*)
*Open: Tue–Sun 10am–6pm, Closed: Mon.*
Stay the night in Kaunas (*see accommodation listings p172*).
**Day 4:** Leave for Klaipėda in the morning. Spend the afternoon exploring the Curonian Spit (*see drive p106*).
**Day 5:** Travel north to the seaside resort of Palanga (*see walk p96*). In the afternoon, either laze on the beach or if you're feeling like a trip in the car, drive to the Hill of Crosses (*see pp109–12*). Stay the night in Palanga (*see accommodation listings p173*).
**Day 6:** Drive back to Vilnius, enjoying the beautiful scenery on the way. In the evening, treat yourself to a farewell meal in one of the many fine restaurants Vilnius has to offer (*see directory pp164–7*). Stay the night in Vilnius.
**Day 7:** Depart in the morning for home.

### Baltish
Baltish is the clash of English with the Baltic languages, in which there are normally no survivors! Places to look out for Baltish are menus in restaurants, signs in hotel rooms, street signs converted directly from the local language into English and local tourist information translated into English.

# Vilnius

When Lithuania regained its independence in 1991 after many centuries of occupation and destruction, Vilnius once again became the capital and centre of the nation. Since then it has been undergoing a huge programme of restoration and development and is emerging as a multi-cultural European city of magnificent buildings and thriving enterprise. With Lithuania becoming a fully-fledged member of NATO and the European Union in 2004, the relaunch of its capital was given a further boost.

A view of the River Neris from the Higher Castle

Vilnius has been the heart of Lithuania since the city was founded by Duke Gediminas in the 14th century (*see p12*). However, it had been a settlement since 2500–2000 BC, long before the formal founding of the city by the Grand Duke.

The Gates of Dawn, a well-known Vilnius landmark, that gives this street its name
Aušros Vartų gatvė

The city's fortunes have always faithfully mirrored the country's. Throughout Lithuania's fractured and turbulent history, including the Lithuanian–Polish Commonwealth that spanned the 17th and 18th centuries, annexation by Russia and Poland at various times, and occupation by Germany, Poland and Russia, Vilnius was one of the cities to bear the brunt of the downswings. When Lithuania finally attained its independence and the economic, cultural and social revival of the country began, Vilnius was the first to benefit.

The city stands at the confluence of the Neris (also called the Vilija) and Vilnia rivers, with hills rising from the riverbanks. Gediminas Hill, at 48m, is the highest of these and is the seat of Vilnius's great landmark, the Higher Castle.

### Aukštutinės Pilies Muziejus (Higher Castle Museum)

All that remains of Gediminas Castle, built between the 13th and 15th centuries, is the three-storey defence tower known as Gediminas Tower. Built Gothic-style on an octagonal plan in red brick, the tower now houses a museum with displays on Vilnius's medieval fortification system, swords, armour and ancient coins. However, the best reason to come up here is for the great views. *Castle Hill, Arsenalo 5. Open: Tue–Sun 10am–5pm. Tel: (370 5) 261 74 53; Admission charge. The funicular railway will save you the climb.*

## Aušros Vartų (Gates of Dawn)

A famous symbol of the city of Vilnius, the Gates of Dawn were built into the city wall in the 16th century as part of the city's original fortification. One of the finest Renaissance pieces in the city, the Gates were used to mark the eastern entrance to Vilnius. Since the expansion of the city, the Gates are now positioned in the centre.

In 1671, the Carmelites from nearby St Theresa's built a chapel at the Gates to house a holy image of the Virgin Mary. The most famous image of the Madonna in Lithuanian art, the *Mother of Compassion* painting is supposed to possess healing power. Another special feature of this painting is that it is one of only five celebrated paintings of Holy Mary in Lithuania where she is represented without the baby Jesus. The Madonna is considered to be a symbol of harmony and a special patron of Lithuania as she is worshipped by two religions – Catholics and Orthodox – and four nationalities –

## Vilnius City

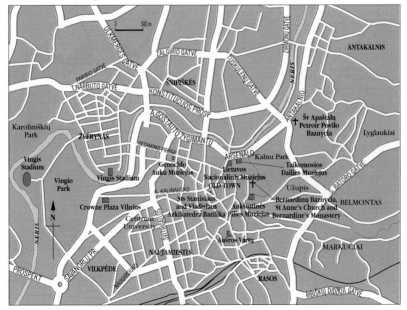

Lithuanians, Poles, Russians and Belarusians.

The chapel spreads across the top of the arch and you can see the image of the Virgin Mary as you approach the Gates from the west. Take time to go into the chapel – the interior was refurbished in neo-Classical style in 1829 and is well worth a look.
*Aušros Vartų gatvė 12.*
*Tel: (370 5) 212 35 13; Open: daily.*

**Bernardinų Baznycia (Bernardine Church), St Anne's Church and Bernardine's Monastery**

This unusual group of buildings on the eastern edge of the Old Town makes an extraordinary Gothic composition. St Anne's Church, which is the smallest of the three buildings, was built in the late 15th century and is considered the most famous late-Gothic building in Lithuania. It is believed to have been

Thirty-three different varieties of brick were used on the façade of St Anne's Church

The Cathedral and Belfry are a landmark and meeting place in the city

designed by Benedikt Rejt, who was also the architect of the Vladislav Hall in Hradčany, Prague. Its striking dark-red brick façade is a complex construction of 33 different varieties of bricks, combined to create a fine and elegant exterior. A much-quoted story describes how Napoleon Bonaparte was so impressed by the building that he wanted to take it back to Paris on the palm of his hand. The reality of his connection with the church is more prosaic – he used the church to house his cavalry, who are said to have burnt some of the intricate carved-wood furniture to keep themselves warm.

The Bernardinų Baznycia (Bernardine Church), in contrast to St Anne's, is one of the largest Gothic churches in Lithuania. Although predominantly Gothic in style, the Bernardine Church had some Renaissance and baroque features added in the 17th and 18th centuries after it was damaged by fire and war. It was abandoned as a place of worship during Soviet occupation and handed over to an art institute, the Brothers of St Francis only returning in 1994.

*The complex is on 8/10 Maironio gatvė.*

### Genocido Auku Muziejus (The Museum of Genocide Victims)

You get an inkling of what is to come as you approach this museum. The wall is covered with names carved into the

The fine 18th-century New Arsenal now houses the National Museum

stone. These are the victims of genocide who went into this prison and never come out. This former KGB prison, in use until August 1991, when the KGB left Lithuania, is more or less as it was then. The only difference is that there are printed explanations outside the rooms, describing their function.

The jail was equipped in the autumn of 1940, soon after the Soviet Union occupied Lithuania. Beds and the occasional chair were added much later. Prior to that, inmates were packed into the cells – up to 40 in one cell – allowing only standing room.

You descend into the dimly lit basement with an audio tape that lasts about 50 minutes. As you go from cell to cell, a matter-of-fact description of the horrors that took place regularly in these cells keeps pace.

There is a grim aspect to every cell. Visitors are taken through 19 common wards or cells as well as some of the specialised rooms: the room of the officer on duty, with the equipment used in 1975; a watchroom with Soviet officers' uniforms; and a tiny library that was made available to prisoners only in the 1980s. There's the cell for inquisitions, the padded cell, the isolation cell, and – one of the most sobering – the water-torture or wet punishment cells. Here prisoners were left naked for hours on end, with frequent administrations of icy water keeping them awake.

The passage stretches on bleakly, with

cells off it to right and left. Several contain themed exhibitions listing, with photographs, some of the KGB officers who presided over the jail or directed its operations. At the end of the corridor, there is a cell where prisoners were executed, with a glass-panelled floor and accompanying exhibition. It makes for a bizarre experience to realise that below your feet you can see the remains and intimate possessions of those who were executed here. On the ground floor, there is a detailed exhibition on the oppression of Lithuania under occupying regimes (1940–1990). Material on and photographs of the anti-Soviet and anti-Nazi resistance are displayed, with stories and profiles of the participants. There is a particularly moving account of the Siberian deportations.

*Auku gatvė 2a/ Gedimino pr. 42. Tel: (370 5) 249 74 27; www.genocid.lt. Open: Tue–Sat 10am–5pm, Sun 10am–3pm. Admission charge.*

### Lietuvos Nacionalinis Muziejus (Lithuanian National Museum)

A visit to this museum is an excellent way to get a handle on Lithuanian social history and culture. The extensive exhibits show the minutiae of daily living from the 13th century to the present day, and are constantly updated. Some of the earliest Lithuanian coins, discovered as recently as 2002 around the site of the Lower Castle, are now on display at the museum.

*Arsenalo 1. Tel: (370 5) 262 94 26; email: muziejus@lnm.lt; www.lnm.lt. Open: Tue–Sat 10am–5pm, Sun 10am–3pm. Admission charge.*

### Pilies Gatvė (Pilies Street)

One of the oldest streets in Vilnius, this used to run from the southern gate of

The lovely leafy surroundings of St Paraskeva off Pilies gatvė

the Lower Castle all the way to the Town Hall. Today, the southern gate is less obvious and you reach Pilies gatvė across the eastern end of Cathedral Square. It is now Pilies gatvė only as far as the Russian Orthodox Church **St Paraskeva**, where it becomes Didžioji gatvė, which in turn becomes Aušros Vartų gatvė, leading up to the Gates of Dawn.

Pilies gatvė is very much a commercial street, with some charming ancient lanes leading off it on both sides: to the right S Skapo gatvė and Šv Jono gatvė, (*see Walk pp52–3*) and to the left Bernardinų, Šv Mylo and Literatu. It is worth diving down some of these lanes as they contain some beautiful buildings and charming hidden courtyards. Some of the magnificent structures on

## GREEN BRIDGE

The Green Bridge contains the only four Soviet monuments left in Vilnius. There are four statues on the four corners of the bridge, which are four symbols representing the communist regime. These are the icons of a farmer, a worker, a solider and a student. You cross the Green Bridge from the city centre to get to the church of St Peter and St Paul, an essential site in Vilnius. The Green Bridge runs across the River Neris, the second largest river in Lithuania. However, it is also one of the most polluted, so going swimming or fishing is not recommended!

Church of St Peter & St Paul – a favourite stop on the city bus tour

Pilies gatvė still have their original stairways and elaborate decoration.

Trade was always the main function of this area and it is still Vilnius's most popular shopping neighbourhood. The lofty arcades of some of the old buildings now house outdoor market stalls, selling a range of local and tourist-oriented items. The street has a wide range of upmarket shops, embassies, cultural centres and museums, as well as a plethora of cafés, bars and restaurants.

## Sts Stanislaus and Vladislaus Arkikatedra Bazilika (Arch-Cathedral Basilica of St Stanislaus and St Vladislaus)

One of the best-known and most important buildings in Vilnius, the Cathedral gives its name to the square on which it is situated, the city's most popular meeting place. The Cathedral site is thought to date back to pagan times when, it is believed, a sacred fire or an altar was located here. It is generally agreed that Grand Duke Mindaugas built the first cathedral on this site after being baptised in 1251. The current building dates back to 1419, but the Cathedral has been reconstructed and renovated several times following fire and natural damage,

The Grim Reaper wails from an alcove in the Church of St Peter and St Paul

and features some Renaissance and baroque elements.

Much of what we see today dates from work carried out in 1820 by the architect Laurynas Stuoka-Gucevicius, after severe damage by a storm in 1769, which destroyed the south tower of the façade. During the 1950s the Soviets

### Vilnius Tourist Information

The main tourist centres in the city are at:
*Didžioji g 31, LT-01128 Vilnius.*
*Tel: (370 5) 262 64 70.*
*Vilniaus g 22, LT-01119 Vilnius.*
*Tel: (370 5) 262 96 60.*
*Gelezinkelio g 16, LT-02100 Vilnius.*
*Tel: (370 5) 269 20 91.*
or log onto *www.vilnius.lt*

### Vilnius Churches

For those particularly interested in the churches of Vilnius, which number over a hundred, there is a guide that concentrates on the churches alone. This comprehensive and useful guide comes with a map of the Old Town on which all the churches are located. Six recommended walking routes guide you through the most impressive Gothic, 17th-century, baroque and Orthodox churches. *Vilnius Churches: A Guide, Katalikų pasaulio leidiniai, 2005.* ISBN 9955-619-50-3. Price: 12.13lt

closed the Cathedral as a religious centre and used it as a picture gallery and organ concert venue.

There are 11 chapels in this superb structure, of which the High baroque **St Casimir's Chapel**, created in 1636 to house the sarcophagus of Lithuania's patron saint St Casimir, is regarded as a national treasure. The **Wollowicz Chapel** is also considered to be of high artistic merit. St Casimir's coffin was housed in here until it moved to the eponymous chapel in 1636. St Casimir features again on the pediment of Wollowicz Chapel, along with sculptures of two other saints, St Stanislav and St Helena. These represent the painstaking craft of restorers working from photographs to recreate the three original statues of the saints, which were torn down and

discarded by the Soviets in 1950. *Katedros 1. Tel: (370 5) 261 11 27. Open: Mass daily 6pm and 7pm; Sat 8am, 9am, 6pm and 7pm; Sun 10am–2pm on the hour, 6pm and 7pm.*

**The Belfry**, a free-standing building 57m high, was originally built as the defensive tower of the Lower Castle. The base of the tower dates from the 13th century and the round mid-section from the 14th century. Work began on transforming the tower into a belfry in 1522, and even though it has a mixture of baroque (the first two tiers) and Classical (third one) styles, the result is harmonious.

Ten of the bells in the belfry were cast between the 16th and 18th centuries by famous masters. In 1967, 17 new bells were added, and six more were received

Tryų Kryžių Kalnas (Hill of Three Crosses)

in 2002. Keep your ears open for the tolls ringing out over the city every 15 minutes.

The imposing monument to Gediminas, the founder of Vilnius, was erected in 1996 and dominates the castle end of the square. Viewed against a darkening sky, the statue looks particularly dramatic.

### Šv Apaštalų Petroir Povilo Baznycia (Church of St Peter and St Paul)

Michael Casimir Pac, the Grand Hefman of the Lithuanian armies, commissioned the building of this church in 1668 but unfortunately died before it was completed. The exterior of the church is impressive and attractive, but nothing to match the fabulous baroque interior. Look to the right as you enter the church and you can see his tombstone embedded in the wall. Also note the figure of the Grim Reaper lurking in the alcove to the right just as you enter the church. The stucco figures number over two thousand and represent various Biblical, theological and battle scenes. An unusual and striking feature of the church is the huge ship-shaped chandelier that was made especially for the church of brass and glass beads in Latvia.
*Antakalnio 1. Tel: (370 5) 234 02 29. Services: daily morning and evening, three services on Sun; services conducted in Lithuanian and Polish.*

### Taikomosios Dailies Muziejus (Applied Art Museum)

Housed in the Old Arsenal of the Lower Castle, this museum exhibits applied and religious art spanning the 14th to the 20th centuries.

The Belfry's soft coloured stone is highlighted in the evening light

*Arsenalo 3a. Tel: (370 5) 262 80 80, 261 25 48; www.ldm.lt. Open: Tue–Sat 11am–6pm, Sun 11am–4pm. Admission charge.*

### Tryu Kryžių Kalnas (Hill of Three Crosses)

High up on the hill on the opposite bank of the River Vilnia from Gediminas Castle, you can see three distinctive white crosses. Legend tells how centuries ago, seven Franciscan monks were crucified here and the bodies of four thrown into the Vilnia. Originally erected in the 17th century as symbols of mourning and hope, these crosses were removed and buried on Stalin's orders. The ones we see

The buildings of Vilnius University line the small curved streets in this part of the Old Town

You can admire the intricate and detailed carving on the old University doorway

today were rebuilt to the original specifications and erected in 1989. They are impressive both from a distance and up close, and it is worth the climb to their feet to enjoy another excellent view of the Old Town.

### Kazys Varnelis House-Museum

As a painter Kazys Varnelis (1917–) has incorporated a number of styles in his art, with the overall effect of geometric compositions. He studied Applied and Decorative Arts in Kaunas but managed to escape the Soviet occupation in 1949 by going to the USA. He contributed much to the art movement in America and his work features in some of the better known art galleries and museums across the United States. Varnelis amassed a formidable and quite eccentric collection of art, sculpture, furniture, books and oddities dating from the 14th century. In 1998 when

Lithuania regained its independence, Kazys Varnelis and his wife returned to Lithuania with their collection and donated it to the state. Together with the Ministry of Culture and the Vilnius Academy of Fine Art, the Varnelis's set up this highly original museum which is well worth a visit not only for the pieces themselves but also for being the collection of one individual.

*Didžioji gatvė 26. Tel: (370 5) 279 16 44; www.lnm.lt. Open by appointment only, Tue–Sat 10am–5pm. Admission free.*

## Vilniaus Gatvė
## (Vilniaus Street)

Linking Vokiečių gatvė (*see pp50–51*) to Gedimino Prospektas, Vilniaus gatvė is a continuation of Vokiečių gatvė and one of the major city streets, culminating at Zaliasis Bridge.

One of the most impressive buildings on this street is Radziwill Palace, at Nos 39–41. There were originally three houses on this site, which were joined together in the 17th century to form the palace, where both baroque and Renaissance features are evident. The main Vilnius City Theatre was based here from 1796 to 1810. When it relocated to the Town Hall, other smaller

theatre companies used it as a venue till the 1840s. The theatrical connection is still alive – the structure now houses the Lietuvos Teatro, Muzikos, Kino Muziejus (Theatre, Music and Film Museum).

*Vilniaus gatvė 41. Tel: (370 5) 262 24 06. Open: Tue–Fri noon–6pm, Sat 11am–4pm. Admission charge.*

## Vilniaus Universitetas
## (Vilnius University)

The university is contained within four streets: Pilies gatvė to the east, S. Skapo gatvė to the north, Universiteto gatvė to

St Theresa's Church in Aušros Vartų gatvė

Evening sun lights up some of the fine University buildings

the west and Šv Jono gatvė to the south and Daukanto Square. There are some other university buildings dotted around the Old Town, but it is this main area that contains the finest buildings and the most intense history.

The oldest university in Eastern Europe, Vilniaus Universitetas features examples of every major architectural style from the last 400 years. The beginnings of the University date from 1568, when Bishop Walerian Protasewicz purchased a two-storey Gothic house in the area. This was later taken over by the Jesuit order which founded the university in 1579 and ran it for the next 200 years. From this relatively small

building, the ensemble grew, with 12 more buildings added in the area. The Russians closed the university in 1832, and it was reopened only in 1919. A tremendous renovation effort was then carried out on the buildings. Completed in 1979, it made the university buildings among the best preserved in the city. Each of the buildings has a number of wings, and are set around courtyards of various dimensions. The complex is a wonderful place to soak up the atmosphere of the various courtyards and arcades.

There are a range of halls and fine rooms inside these grand buildings that are well worth visiting, with the

library affording one of the most interesting architectural and impressive sections of the university; Smuglewicz Hall is one of the finest examples of architecture.
*Universiteto gatvė 3.*

### Vokiečių Gatvė (Vokiečių Street)

Another of the ancient streets of Vilnius, dating back to the 14th century, it was named after German craftsmen and merchants who set up shop here. The street's heyday was in the 16th century, when the wealthiest merchants built the grandest masonry houses along the street. Vokiečių gatvė continued to be a commercial centre up to the advent of the Second World War with, somewhat unusually, the large shops more likely to be found on the first floors of the big houses, and smaller ones tucked into courtyards and archways.

After the Second World War, the Soviets decided to redevelop the street and razed the half-destroyed eastern side of the street to the ground, creating a grand wide road that bisected the Old Town up to Zaliasis Bridge. Over a period of time, the road was widened four times, and many monuments and fine buildings were destroyed in the process. With only the old buildings on the western side surviving, the contrast is very clear today.

One of the most impressive buildings is Tyzenhaus, the Wittinghoff estate at No 28. This is a historic site with grand buildings dating back to 1597. It was reconstructed a number of times over the years, but the magnificent Classical façade we see today was the work of Martin Knackfull, a popular period architect. The building was renovated most recently in the 1950s to repair the damage occasioned by the Second World War.

Notice the contrasting architecture of this main thoroughfare

# Walk: Vilnius: Circular Walk from Cathedral Square

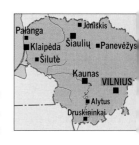

This easy ramble charts a circular route around Vilnius Old Town. It will take you through a mixture of main thoroughfares and quieter backstreets, giving you a chance to get a quick sense of the history and atmosphere.

*Time: Allow about three hours for the full walk, which will give you a chance to take the occasional break.*

*Distance: 3km.*

*The walk begins in Cathedral Square.*

## 1 Katedros Aikštė (Cathedral Square)

This is the focal point of the Old Town. Part of the present structure dates back to 1419 but additions and reconstructions were carried out between 1769 and 1820 (*see p44*). There are 11 chapels within the vast cathedral worth visiting, with St Casimir's High baroque chapel being one of the most impressive. Beside the cathedral is the unusual free-standing bell tower. The imposing statue of Grand Duke Mindaugas was added after Lithuania regained its independence.

*Head south across the square down Pilies gatvė. You may take a short detour off the gatvė to visit some of the historic lanes along it. From Pilies gatvė, turn right down Skapo gatvė and into Universiteto gatvė to reach Vilnius Universitetas.*

## 2 Vilnius Universitetas (Vilnius University)

Founded in 1579, the oldest university in Eastern Europe comprises many

fine buildings, incorporating 400 years of architectural styles (*see pp49–50*). It is worth wandering around the courtyards and seeing some of the interiors.

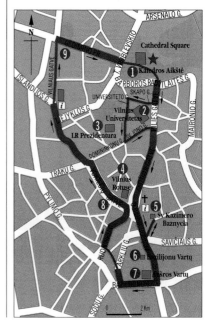

*Walk across Universiteto gatvė to
LR Prezidentura.*

### 3 LR Prezidentura
### (Presidential Palace)

Originally built for the city's Bishop in
the 14th century and remodelled in the
early 19th century, it has had various
occupants since, including Tsar Alexander
I and Napoleon Bonaparte. It became
the Artists' Palace during the Soviet
occupation and currently contains the
offices of the President.

*Continue along Universiteto gatvė (leaving
the university buildings on your left) until
you reach the junction of Šv Jono gatvė.
Turn left down Šv Jono gatvė and right to
rejoin Pilies gatvė. Pilies gatvė becomes
Didžioji gatvė; continue along this road till
you reach the Town Hall.*

### 4 Vilnius Rotuse (Town Hall)

Now the Artists' Palace, this classical
structure, complete with Doric portico,
was redesigned from a 15th-century
structure by Laurynas Stuoka-Gucevicius
between 1781 and 1799. It was used as a
theatre for over a century up until 1924
when it became the Lithuanian Art
Museum under Soviet occupation.

*Take the road off to the southeast corner
of the Town Hall, continuing along
Šv Kazimero and Aušros Vartų gatvė.*

### 5 Šv Kazimero Baznycia (St Casimir)

This baroque church is named after the
patron saint of Lithuania, St Casimir.
Used as a grain store by Napoleon's
troops in 1812, it was converted into a
cathedral by the Russians in 1864 and
finally into a Museum of Aetheism
under the Soviets before being returned

to its original use after independence.

*Continue along Aušros Vartų gatvė until
you reach Bazilijonu Vartų on the right-
hand side of the road.*

### 6 Bazilijonu Vartų (Basilian Gate)

This fabulous baroque gateway serves as
the entrance to the Basilian monastery.
Built in 1761 to a grand design, it looks
somewhat incongruous today alongside
the rather dilapidated church.

*Continue along Aušros Vartų gatvė until
you reach Aušros Vartų.*

### 7 Aušros Vartų (Gates of Dawn)

These famous gates are a Vilnius
landmark (*see pp39–40*).

*Go through the Gates of Dawn, turn right
down Bazilijonu gatvė, take the first right
down Sventutujus gatvė, and then third
right down Rudninku gatvė. This brings
you back to the Town Hall. Turn left into
Vokiečių gatvė.*

### 8 Vokiečių Gatvė

This wide street has a chequered history.
You can guess at its former glory from
the fine buildings that remain on the
eastern side (*see pp50–51*).

*At the end of Vokiečių gatvė is the junction
of Trakų and Domininkonu gatvės. Head
straight across down Vilniaus gatvė and
continue along the road until it
culminates at Gedimino Prospektas.*

### 9 Gedimino Prospektas

Named after the Lithuanian Grand
Duke the street reflects the new identity,
with large stores, banks and hotels.

*If you return to Gedimino pr. and walk
back down in an easterly direction, you
will eventually reach Cathedral Square.*

# Walk: Vilnius Old Town

This is more of a scenic walk punctuated with some important sights than a purely cultural experience. It is a walk that is geared towards vistas – along the River Neris and two opportunities to look out over the city and experience Vilnius from a different perspective.

*Allow 3 hours.*

*Distance: 4km.*

*Start the walk at the Green Bridge.*

## 1 Zaliasis Tiltas (Green Bridge)

Zaliasis Tiltas or the Green Bridge links the New Town to the Snipiskes district. Start from the Snipiskes side and cross over the River Neris, which is the second biggest in Lithuania. Unfortunately it is one of the most polluted, so don't be tempted to swim or fish in it. The Green Bridge contains the only four monuments left in Vilnius from the Soviet era. There is a statue on each of the four corners of the bridge representing symbols of communist times, namely a farmer, a worker, a solider and a student. These are described as social realist sculptures.

*Cross over Green Bridge and go straight across Zygimantu down Vilniaus gatvė till it reaches the junction of Gedimino Prospektas.*

## 2 Gedimino Prospektas

Time spent on Gedimino Prospektas will vary depending on the needs of the walkers – whether it be shopping, culture or simply the need for a beer – you can find all this close at hand (*see p53*).

*Go down Gedimino Prospektas and into Cathedral Square.*

## 3 Arkikatedra Bazilika (The Cathedral) (*see pp45–7*)

*Head northeast from Cathedral Square down Sventaragio T. Vrublevsklo. When you reach the river, turn right into Arsenalo T. Kosciuskos. On your right is the Lithuanian National Museum.*

## 4 Lietuvos Nacionalinis Muziejus (Lithuanian National Museum)

There is a huge collection of items in this museum, ranging from books, coins, weapons and prints to pieces of architectural interest, folk art and findings from the mass graves of soldiers

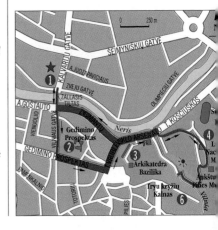

of Napoleon's retreating army. You certainly come away with a feel of what Lithuania and its people are all about.
*Just next door to the museum is the entrance to the funicular railway that will take you up to the Higher Castle.*

## 5 Aukštutinės Pilies Muziejus (Higher Castle Museum)

You can explore the castle ruins and the tower (*see pp38–9*).
*Make your way back down the hill by foot. It is an attractive walk down the cobbled roadway, but make sure you are wearing shoes with the ability to grip: even when dry, the smooth cobbles are slightly slippery. From Kalnu Park at the foot of the castle, you cross the small Vilnia River and walk on to Tryu Kryžių Kalnas (Hill of Three Crosses).*

This short funicular railway saves you the climb to the Higher Castle

## 6 Tryu Kryžių Kalnas (Hill of Three Crosses)

Check out the crosses from up close (*see pp47–8*) and enjoy the stunning vista from the hill.

The three-storey defence tower known as Gediminas Tower, is all that is left of the Higher Castle

Close to the centre of Vilnius, across the River Vilnia, is the 'Republic of Uzupis'. First mentioned in the 16th century, the Uzupis quarter was a residential area for the poor. However, over the years, it became a popular place to live for students, poets, romantics and artists. The prices of the houses here began to rise considerably and, in 1998, the citizens of this bohemian district declared it a 'break-away Republic'.

Uzupis has become a centre for non-conventional ideas. Not only does it have its own road signs, but also its own Constitution, a President, Ministers, an Ambassador in Moscow, and its own public holidays. The most popular of these holidays is on 1st April, Uzupis' 'Day of Independence', when a 'visa' is required for entry into this area and fake border policemen in silly costumes guard the border, checking and stamping the passports. A variety of strange events takes place on this Day of Independence, including the central water pump becoming a 'beer pump'. Other holidays in Uzupis include the 'Day of the River' on 24th July, the 'Night of the Flowers' on 15th August, and the 'Day of the Idiot' on 21st

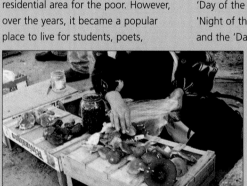

September. The Constitution contains plenty of strange articles, including such gems as 'Every dog has the right to be a dog'. The Constitution ends with 'Don't conquer, Don't defend, Don't surrender' (see box for more extracts from Uzupis' Constitution).

In the centre of the area, where the two main streets

scientists can be found in this peaceful spot. Close to the Bernardine Church and cemetery is the Fluxus Bridge, named after the group that tried to blow up the bridge in order to destroy the border between art and life!

of Malūno and Paupio intersect, there is a tall pillar on which sits the statue of the famous Uzupis angel. This is a beautiful figure of an angel blowing her trumpet. When the Dalai Lama, who has been granted honorary citizenship of Uzupis, visited the area, he declared that he wanted the angel's horn to sound across the earth. Before the Day of Independence of 2002, there was a giant egg here that represented the 'rebirth' that was taking place in this part of this city. Supposed to have given birth to the beautiful angel, the egg is now displayed in a different part of the city. Artists have placed other similar figures around Vilnius' main city squares.

The old Bernardine cemetery that stretches along the steep riverside at the southeastern end of the district has become a mystical location in Uzupis. Burials began here in 1810, and during the 1863 uprising, rebels hid their weapons here. The gravestones of many Vilnius University professors and

Facing page above: A close-up of the Uzupis Angel; below: Selling mushrooms from a makeshift street stall
This page above: Graffiti in the bohemian 'Republic' of Uzupis

### EXCERPTS FROM THE UZUPIS CONSTITUTION

- Man has the right to make mistakes.
- Man has the right to be unique.
- Man has the right to live beside the River, and Vilna (the river) has the right to flow beside the man.
- Man has the right to be not famous or unknown.
- Man has the right to love.
- Man has the right to be loved, but not necessarily.
- Man has the right to love and care for a cat.
- A cat is not obliged to love its owner but during hard times it is obliged to help the owner.
- Man has the right to care for a dog until one of them passes away.

# Around Vilnius

For travellers who have plenty of time in Vilnius or feel a bit more adventurous, there are many sights to explore on the outskirts of the city. Some are close enough to walk to, others a short bus ride away; all are reachable by car. Guided bus tours to Trakai and Europos Parkas generally leave in the morning and take around three and a half hours. They'll pick you up and return you to your hotel.

Yachts for hire by the entrance of the Island Castle at Trakai

**Belmontas Recreation Centre**
Close to the Pavilniai Regional Park, this entertainment and recreation centre has a swimming pool, leisure centre and restaurants.
*Belmonto g 17. Tel: (370 8) 615 20 220. www.belmontas.lt*

**Pavilniai Regional Park**
This attractive regional park close to Vilnius has been created to preserve both the nature and culture of Lithuania. One of the most interesting aspects of the park is the different levels throughout that vary by up to 100m. Situated within the park is the most interesting rock structure, the Puckoriai, which is one of the highest in the country. Around 65m high, the rock measures 260m in width. It is worth climbing to the top of the rock to enjoy the panorama of the Vilnia river valley. From here you can walk to a watermill

**Travel Information**
For information on schedules for organised bus tours and excursions to the sights within and around Vilnius, contact any tourist information office in the city centre.

complex and the ruins of the Puckoriai canon foundry.
*Zaliuju Ezery g 53. Tel: (370 2) 72 98 34; www.pavilniai-verkiai.lt. Admission free.*

**Puškino Memorialinis Muziejus (Pushkin Memorial Museum)**
In the Markuciai Reserve in another area of the park is the Puškino Memorialinis Muziejus. Although the connection is pretty close, it was actually Alexander Pushkin's son and his wife rather than the poet himself who lived in this interesting wooden house on their estate from 1899 to 1935. The house was turned into a museum dedicated to the famous Russian poet in 1940, opening in 1948.
*Subaciaus 124. Tel: (370 5) 260 00 80. Open: Wed–Sun 10am–5pm. Admission free.*

**Paneriai**
A very different experience from visiting the above estate, Paneriai is located about 10km southwest of the centre of the city. This infamous forested site is where the Nazis and a number of Lithuanian recruits murdered over

100,000 people during the Second World War (*see p15*). Among those murdered and thrown into the oil storage pits that the Nazis inherited from the Soviets were people brought here from all over Europe. The area, known as the 'killing grounds', is about a 1km walk into the woods from the train station. There are two stones marking the entrance to the site, which were erected after the war by the communists and simply tabulate the Soviet citizens who were murdered.

The reality was that over 70,000 of the 100,000 killed were Jews, and the memorial erected in 1990 makes this clear with its inscription in Hebrew. It is still possible to see the remains of the barracks and the pits.

The **Panerių Memorialinis Muziejus**

(Paneriai Memorial Museum) has a small but graphically informative display showing the atrocities that happened here and the chilling description of the Nazis later attempts to cover up the evidence. The building was purpose-built in 1965 to provide a memorial museum for those who died. In addition to the main exhibition, personal items of the victims including pictures and documents dug up at the site are on display.

*Agrastu gatvė 15. Tel: (370 5) 260 20 01; Open: Mon, Wed–Fri noon–6pm, Sat & Sun 11am–6pm.*

*Directions: Take a suburban train (direction SW) from Vilnius station to Paneriai. From the station at Paneriai, turn right on Agrastu gatvė, following the road for 1km through the woods.*

## Around Vilnius

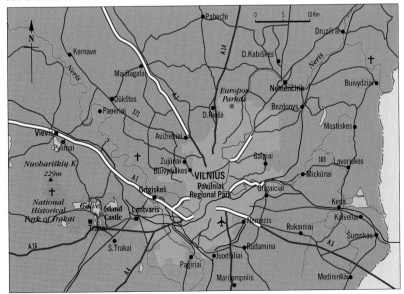

## Rumšiškės

The village of Rumšiškės is only 13km east of Kaunas but constitutes an easy day-trip from Vilnius. The village has an extremely attractive setting on the banks of the River Nemunas. Archaeologists have found bronze artefacts here dating from the 13th to the 16th centuries AD. The village has become almost synonymous with the Open-Air Museum of Lithuania, which is actually some 5km further east.

### Rumšiškės Open-Air Museum of Lithuania

Spread over 176ha, or 435 acres, the site comprises workplaces, dwelling houses and other representative buildings brought here from different regions of the country – Lithuania Minor, Suvalkija, Žemaitija (Lower Lithuania or Samogitia) and Aukštaitija (Upper Lithuania). These assorted structures, laid out across the park, represent the most characteristic stylistic features of buildings from different historical eras. The huge collection of over 80,000 items includes furniture, household items, beehives, orchards and other artefacts. The aim of the museum is to illustrate the way of life, work and traditions of the Lithuanian

**The Karaites**
The Karaites originally came from the Byzantine Empire in Mesopotamia in the 8th century, and then moved into the Crimean Peninsula, from where Grand Duke Vytautas brought them to Trakai in the 15th century. The word Karaite comes originally from Arabic and the Hebrew word 'kara' translates as 'reading the scriptures'. There are currently around 250 Karaites still living in Lithuania, mainly in Trakai and Vilnius.

people, both urban and rural, over the last hundred years.
*56km west of Vilnius on the Kaunas–Vilnius motorway. S. Neries g 6, Rumšiškės, Kaisiadorys district. Tel: (370 346) 472 33. Open: Tue–Sun, 10am–6pm. Closed: Mon. Admission charge.*

### Televizljos Bokštas (Television Tower)

Although the building itself is not one of particular architectural note it is its historical associations that make it an interesting place to visit. On January 13th 1991 in an attempt to prevent Lithuania achieving its independence, the Soviet Army tanks surrounded the Television Tower and tried to occupy the main government buildings. The army faced hundreds of unarmed civilians and during the clash 14 Lithuanians were killed. There are poignant monuments to those who died outside the tower and inside is a small exhibition of photographs recording the unforgettable event. The tower itself at 326m is higher than the Eiffel Tower in Paris and you can get great views of the city from the café at the top of the tower on a clear day and at night.

**Trakai Tourist Information**
This should be one of your first ports of call in the town. The centre has a plethora of information and maps, as well as extremely helpful and informative staff.
*Vytauto g 69. Tel: (370 528) 51 934; email: trakaiTIC@is.lt; www.trakai.lt.*
*Open: May–Sept Mon 8.30am–4.15pm, Tue–Fri 8.30am–5.30pm, Sat 9am–3pm. Closed for lunch noon–12.45pm.*

Colourful houses in Karaimu gatvė with their mystical messages of three windows

*Sausio 13 Oslos 10. Tel: (370 5) 252 53 33; www.lrtc.lt. Open: daily 10am–10pm.*

## Trakai

Trakai is both a region and the name of the main town in the region. The Trakai district, with a population of around 38,000, is well known for its lakes, which number over 300, and over 200 agricultural, natural and cultural monuments.

Situated 28km from Vilnius, Trakai is famous both within Lithuania and abroad for its beautiful surroundings and historic sights, including a charming village and a most spectacular castle on an island in one of the many lakes in the area.

The town is spread down either side of the main street with a concentration of tourist shops and cafés in the centre, from where you embark on your walk across the various islands to reach the Island Castle. It is a quiet place with a somewhat otherworldly air. This is reinforced by the view across Lake Galve to the wonderful Gothic castle, which looks almost as if it is floating on the water.

Trakai was founded in the late 14th century by Grand Duke Kęstutis, when he moved from Old Trakai and took up residence in the peninsular castle built between the lakes of Luka and Galve. Further buildings were constructed and, in time, a whole settlement grew around the castle protected by the surrounding hills. During the late 14th and 15th centuries, Trakai developed as a place of huge strategic importance, becoming the

The fairytale Island Castle on Lake Galve is linked to the mainland by a series of footbridges

administrative and political centre of Lithuania.

Historically, Trakai has been unique in Lithuania for its multicultural character. This was partly due to the Grand Duke Vytautas, who brought the Karaite and Tartar families to Lithuania. The Karaites, originally from Turkey, came initially as slaves but were soon elevated to the status of personal guards to the Grand Duke. Other Karaites followed, and a community was formed and still exists here today. In the 16th century, a number of Jewish families settled here and even today Trakai prides itself on the richness and variety of its culture.

Included within the territory are both the National Historical Park of Trakai and the Aukštadvaris Regional Park.

**The Karaites Ethnographical Exhibition**

The Karaites Ethnographical Exhibition is worth a visit to learn more about the Karaite culture and traditions.

*Karaimu gatvė 22. Open: Wed–Sun summer 10am–7pm; winter 10am–5pm. Tel: (370 528) 58 241. Admission charge.*

**Karaimu Gatvė**

This is an interesting street in Trakai where the Karaites set up their community. They have been living in this northern part of the town since they were brought to Trakai by Grand Duke Vytautas from Crimea. They were treated well and given many privileges. Traditionally, they are excellent craftsmen and this street is particularly distinctive for the unusual architecture of the houses. The back walls of these colourful houses have three windows facing the street. Each window has a purpose – one window for God, one window for Duke Vytautas and the third

**Kibinai**

This is a traditional Karaite dish and is somewhat similar to a Cornish pasty. It consists of a pastry case stuffed with a flavoursome mixture of chopped meat and onions mixed together with rich gravy. They come in a variety of sizes and should be served piping hot.

for the Karaite himself or herself.

**Kenesa**, the Karaite prayer house in Karaimu gatvė, is an 18th-century building distinctive in its eastern-style architecture. There are also two Karaite restaurants in Karaimu gatvė at Nos 65 and 29, serving traditional Karaite dishes including *Kibinai* a particular speciality (*see box*).

### National Historical Park of Trakai

The National Historical Park of Trakai was set up in 1991 and is the only historical park in the country. It is made up of 32 lakes, a bird sanctuary, 3 hydrographical reserves and 2 cultural reserves which incorporate the Old Castle site and the 'New' Castle. It covers over 8,000 hectares and includes in addition to the above areas, the cultural landscape reserve of Užutrakis and the urban reserve of Trakai Old Town.

### Island Castle

The most striking building in Trakai is the Island Castle, the only insular castle in Lithuania and the only water castle in Eastern Europe. It was built by Kęstutis and Vytautas, both Grand Dukes of Lithuania, at the end of the 14th and the beginning of the 15th centuries to a very unusual ground plan. It was strategically set on a relatively inaccessible island in Lake Galve to withstand attacks from

the German crusaders. After the glorious victory of the Lithuanians at the Battle of Grunwald in 1410, Trakai castle became the summer residence of the rulers of the Great Duchy of Lithuania. This was the castle's heyday. Over the ensuing centuries, it suffered great damage and was left in ruins. However, restoration started on it in the 1950s, during the Soviet era, and work continues today. The castle complex is built over three separate islands, and includes a fortress which links to the Gothic Ducal Palace, surrounded by a defensive wall. The main landmark of the complex is the five-storey turret (*donjon*), which rises to 25m. This is linked by a gate to the courtyard of the Palace. There are wooden stairways and balconies connecting the Palace to the Castle, and one of the huge halls on the first floor is still used for concerts and other performances. Some of the other buildings have been converted, and one houses an eclectic collection of historical objects and some pictures tracing the castle's past.

*The approach to the Island Castle is from the town across one wooden bridge, across the tiny Karvine Island and across another wooden bridge to Pilies Salą. Open: daily summer 10am–7pm; winter 10am–5pm. Admission charge.*

### Užutrakis Palace

Situated about 8km southeast of Trakai, still within the National Historical Park, the Užutrakis Palace lies on the northern shore of Lake Galve. The 19th-century manor created by Juozapas Tiškevičius. It was originally designed by the architect Joseph Hus in the Neo-

Sailing boats moored on the lake at Trakai

Classical style and set in a park laid out by the well-known French landscape architect Édouard François André on the shores of Lake Galve. The manor was allowed to deteriorate after the Second World War, but is now being restored.

**Trakai Boat Trip**

Trakai is located on a thin peninsula among three lakes, Galve, Luka and Totoriškių. Although a wonderful place just to wander around, you get a whole different perspective if you explore it from the water.

It is possible to rent your own rowing or paddle boat on Lake Galve, which is the largest of the three lakes. You can also take a guided yacht trip, but we recommend renting your own so long as you feel confident and wear a life jacket.

To the north of the Island Castle on the lake shore, there are a number of outlets renting a variety of boats. Bartering with the boat owners can get you a reasonable price for an hour's rental. Expect to pay up to three times as much for a yacht as for a rowing boat or a canoe.

Touring by boat is a great way to see the Island Castle, which is one of Lithuania's most famous sights. Lake Galve, on which the castle sits, is the most spectacular of the lakes in this area: 46.7m deep and covering 361 hectares, it is both the largest and deepest lake in this region. It is also a designated nature reserve, made up of many peninsulas and bays, which come in various shapes and sizes. There are 21 islands on Lake Galve, most having legends connected to them. There are two islands close to the centre of the lake – the Isle of Wailing (Rauda Salą) and the island of Valka. In the past, people who had been found guilty of a crime and were sentenced to death would be taken to the island of Valka, and their relatives would be taken to the Isle of Wailing. From there they could grimly observe their relatives waiting for their deaths. Castle Island (Pilies Salą) is the largest of the islands.

In the summer months, the lake steamer runs frequent trips from the Island Castle to the northern end of Lake Galve. It is a popular place for hot-air ballooning and paragliding, and there are often competitions taking place here in the summer. Sailing competitions and national and international rowing competitions also take place here. If you are feeling adventurous and want to go cruising a bit further afield, head for Užutrakis Palace (*see pp63–4*) which has a lovely

park and is a great place to stop for a walk and a picnic.

*Rental outlets: Trakai Yacht Club has boats to hire. The Zalgris Yacht Club ((370 528) 52 824, Zemaites gatvė 3) also hire yachts. Trakų Sporto Baze hire speedboats, water bikes, jet skis and regular bicycles ((370 528) 55 501, karaimu gatvė 73).*

The amazing Island Castle in Trakai

M any places in the Continent claim to be the centre of Europe; however, the only one accepted by the Guinness Records Agency is 26km outside Vilnius city, in the direction of Molėtai, near the Purnuskes village. In 1989, a group of scientists from the French National Geographic Institute established Europe's geographical centre using comprehensive contemporary scientific methods. They calculated the centre at 54° 51' North latitude, 25° 19' East longitude, which is here in Lithuania. However, there has recently been some discussion as to whether this

calculation is accurate. The debate continues. While the site is not particularly exciting, it is worth a visit. There is a memorial stone, and an information centre and museum. Visitors can also get certificates to verify that they've been to the centre of Europe.

A more interesting commemoration of the 'centre of Europe' status is Europos Parkas (Park of Europe), a sculpture park that is actually located 14km away from Europe's purported geographical centre. This highly original art museum and park was founded in 1991 by a 23-year-old sculptor student, Gintaras Karosas. Located in a forest 19km north of Vilnius city, the park was established with the aim of underlining the area's status by using the language of art.

The only international contemporary sculpture park in Lithuania, the 55ha Europos Parkas displays non-traditional pieces of work and sculptures by a variety of artists from over 30 countries. The sculptures, representing different cultural traditions and international backgrounds, are on display all year round, with new ones being added from

## THE CENTRE OF EUROPE MUSEUM

T he museum is 26km from Vilnius, towards Molėtai, behind Purnuskes village, Bernotai mound. *Open: Mon–Fri 9am–6pm. Admission free.*

time to time. In 2005, the collection on display in Europos Parkas reached over 100 pieces. The park exhibits large-scale works by famous contemporary artists, including S LeWitt, M Abakanowicz and D Oppenheim.

The largest, and possibly the most well-known, of the pieces is the sculpture *LNK Infotree*, created by Karosas himself. Made of hundreds of used television sets to create a labyrinth in tree form, the sculpture takes up more than 3,135sq m of space. It is not surprising that in 2001 it was officially registered in the Guinness Book of Records as the largest art creation in the world. The pieces *Chair Pool* and *Drinking Structure with Exposed Kidney Pool*, both by Dennis Oppenheim of the USA, are also well known. *Chair Pool*, as its name indicates, is a huge chair with a

pool in the seat. The setting itself is outstanding, with a reservoir, park and wooded hills providing a stunning backdrop for the intriguing sculptures.

Facing page above: Some of the sculptures are interactive; below: Dennis Oppenheim's *Chair Pool*. As the name suggests, a huge chair with a pool in the seat
This page below: the scientifically calculated centre of Europe is marked by this simple pillar

## EUROPOS PARKAS

*Joneikiskių Village, Vilnius area. Tel: (370 5) 2377 077; www.europosparkas.lt*
*Open: daily 9am–sunset. Admission charge.*

Entrance fees are reasonable, with discounted rates for students and pensioners. However watch out for extra costs, such as the fee for taking photos. Guided tours are also available in English, Russian and German. There is a restaurant at the park, with indoor and outdoor seating.

Other services include a souvenir shop and a post office.

To get to Europos Parkas from Vilnius city centre, go down Kalvarijų gatvė up to Santariškių Roundabout, then turn towards the Zalieli Ezerai and follow the signs for the Europos Parkas (Park of Europe). If travelling from the Geographical Centre of Europe, the signs for the Park will lead you down a long and bumpy road. This route should be avoided if possible. There is also a regular bus service from Vilnius city centre.

# Southern Lithuania

The combination of great natural beauty and some fortunate geological features have resulted in a spate of spa towns in Lithuania's picturesque south. Perhaps the most popular of the resort towns is Druskininkai, on the banks of the River Ratnycia. The local mud and mineral springs are believed to have curative powers. The other highly popular resort is Bristonas, where mineral water is the focal point of treatments. There is something to draw nature lovers as well – the Zuvintas Strict State Reserve.

Flowerbeds line the edges of the large parkland area

### Druskininkai

Druskininkai is beautifully located just south of the Nemunas River, about 120km southwest of Vilnius and is surrounded by pine forests filling the air with a clean fresh scent. The town itself is spread over quite a wide area made up of parks and gardens and dotted with lakes. It has a peaceful and unhurried atmosphere making it an ideal place to spend a few days enjoying the scenery, walking in the surrounding forests and

## Southern Lithuania

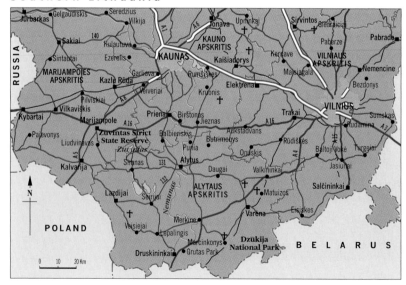

even taking advantage of one of the many spa treatments available in the resort.

One of the oldest and most well-known spas and recreational resorts in Eastern Europe, Druskininkai is located very near the state borders with Poland and Belarus, on the Ratnycia River, close to the Nemunas River. Over the years, the movement of the waves and the accumulation of salts led to the formation of many mineral springs here. The name of the area is derived from the Lithuanian word for salt, 'druska', and 'druskininkas' means 'salt-man'. A salt-man was a person involved in the extraction, selling and delivery of salt.

Traces of habitation going back to the Mesolithic and Neolithic eras have been found in the area. Other archaeological findings include the remains of a defensive castle at the confluence of the Nemunas and Ratnycia rivers. The castle is believed to date from the 13th century, when the Lithuanians were fighting against the Teutonic Order.

The first mention of Druskininkai in written records occurs in the *Lithuanian Metrics*, according to which Druskininkai village was given to the manager of the Pervalkas Manor Voropajus in 1596. The curative powers of the springs near the River Nemunas were discovered by the villagers when they noticed that their ulcerous legs healed faster after they had waded in the waters of the springs. However, Pranas Sūrutis, a folk doctor in the 18th century, was the first to use the mineral springs specifically for healing purposes.

Although Druskininkai did not officially become a spa until 1835, in 1790 King Stanislaus Augustus Poniatowski ordered that the health-giving properties of the mineral waters

Verdant parkland on the edge of Lake Druskonis

of Druskininkai be investigated and in 1794 it was announced by decree that it was a curative locality.

Professor I. Fonberg of Vilnius University published his research on the chemical composition of the mineral water here in 1835. It was this data that made Tsar Nikolai I grant permission for the area to be developed as a spa in 1837.

The development of Druskininkai was assisted by the proximity of the railway line connecting Warsaw and St Petersburg being operational from 1862, and in the late 19th century it was granted town status. It has had some bleak moments since. Suffering in the First World War, it was revived in 1930 and grew from a population of 7,900 that year to 110,000 in 1937. Reconstructive work was carried out in the park in the 1950s, and the resort was tailored during the time of Soviet occupation for the mass treatment of patients from the USSR.

Present-day Druskininkai covers an area of 22 sq km and has a population of around 25,000 people. There are over 11 sanatoria, which provide treatment for virtually all known diseases, with all the experience, research and expertise accumulated over the years. The main treatments use local mineral waters and curative mud, which are ranked among the best in Europe. With an outstanding microclimate, the town also has a lovely and peaceful setting, with pristine lakes and rivers, surrounded by dunes and pine forests. The town itself contains a large green park. The air is pure and clean, scented with the smell of forest flowers. All these factors make this a very special place to visit.

The predominant architectural style is modern and functional but there are a few remarkable 19th century buildings. One of the most remarkable buildings is Staciatikiu cerkve (Russian Orthodox Church). This ornate and flamboyant building with bright blue spires and purple-hued domes sits serenely in the middle of a leafy reservation circled by the resort's traffic. It is worth taking a look inside which is also very much of the same period.

Just off this roundabout you come to the Spa Complex and parkland area with pedestrianised streets, some lined with street stalls as well as more permanent fixtures. Close to the older and somewhat dowdy Spa Complex is the brand new shiny **Gydykla** (Pump Room) with marble floors and a floor-to-ceiling glass room overlooking the park. Shiny modern silver taps dispense the two local spa waters to optimistic visitors.

*Open (Pump Room): daily 8am–8pm. Charge for treatment.*

The central feature of Druskininkai is Lake Druskonis bordered on its northern side by Ciurlionio gatvė. This is one of the main resort roads and runs right the way through the resort. At the turreted Villa Linksma, translating as 'Happy Villa', built in the early 20th century, the Miesto muziejus (Town Museum) has an interesting collection of pictures and other exhibits showing the spa-town life in the 19th century.

*MK Ciurlionio gatvė 59. Tel: (370 313) 510 24. Open: Mon–Sun 11am–5pm. Admission charge.*

On the northern side of Ciurlionio gatvė almost opposite the museum is

The Russian Orthodox Church in Druskininkai

**Šv Mergelės Marijos Škaplierinės baznycia (Church of the Virgin Mary of the Scapular).** This late neo-Gothic church was deisgned by the architect Stephen Schiller.

As you may have gathered from the naming of the main thoroughfare, Mikaloujus Konstantinis Ciurlionis (1875–1911) Lithuania's most famous painter and composer, had a strong connection with Druskininkai having spent part of his early life here. It is fitting that the town should have a museum in his honour. MK Ciurlionis Memorialininis muziejus (MK Ciurlionis Memorial Museum) provides the visitor with a detailed insight into the composer's life. The museum was established in the house where the Ciurlionis family lived. The family had two small houses and there is a recreation of the wooden house that his father bought in the town. It is filled with 19th-century memorabilia and with the piano Ciurlionis's patron Count Oginski had presented him with in 1899 on his graduation from the Warsaw Conservatoire. There is also an interesting display of photographs of various members of the Ciurlionis family. Classical concerts are held in the garden here in summer.
*Ciurlionio gatvė 35.*
*Tel: (370 313) 527 55; Open: Tue–Sun 11am–5pm. Admission charge.*

A few minutes walk up Šv Jokubo gatvė, which leads off Ciurlionio gatvė at the western end of Lake Druskonis, the **Žako Lipšico muziejus (Jacques Lipchitz Museum)** celebrates the life and work of the Lithuanian–Jewish artist and sculptor Jacques Lipchitz

(1891–1973) who was born in Druskininkai. The exhibits are more momentos and contextual exhibits showing the Jewish community in Druskininkai at that time.
*Šv Jokubo gatvė 17.*
*Tel: (370 313) 560 77; Open: Tue–Sat noon–5pm. Admission charge.*

If you head out of town along Ciurlionio gatvė about 1.5km towards Merkine you come to Girios Aidas (Echo of the Forest). This exhibition is housed in a fantastical wooden construction and surrounded by eccentric wooden sculptures at every turn. Wooden snakes lie in the grass, giants stand as pillars of the house and sculptures of birds and animals are tucked into the hollows of trees and dwarves, witches and other fantasy figures are dotted around the grounds. Inside, the exhibition is divided into different sections and parts of the local ecosystem, trees, animals and birds are examined. It is an imaginative, fun and educative place to visit.
*MK Ciurlionio gatvė 102. Tel: (370 313) 539 01; Open: Wed–Sun 10am–6pm. Admission charge.*

**Zuvintas Strict State Reserve**

In addition to the national parks and regional parks, there are four Strict State Reserves, of which Zuvintas Strict State Reserve near Alytus is one of the most attractive. Established in 1937 mainly through the efforts of the naturalist Tadas Ivanauskas (1882–1970), the reserve incorporates Lake Zuvintas and part of the Bukta Forest, and is an important wetland area. It seeks to preserve the area's delicate ecosystem and wildlife, especially the birdlife of the lake and surrounding wetlands.

Spread over an area of 5,440ha, the reserve is 72 per cent wetland and 13 per cent lake. The lake has shallow and silty waters full of submerged plants that thrive in this type of water. There are also many floating islets called *kiniai*. Next to the lake are huge areas of reeds and sedge, particularly favoured by wading birds, as well as two tracts of raised bogs.

The reserve is famed for its birdlife, with an amazing 255 species of birds registered in the reserve. Lake Zuvintas provides a nesting ground for many aquatic birds. The lake is known as the cradle of the Lithuanian swans, because it is from here that they spread to other Lithuanian lakes. Huge flocks of thousands of migrating cranes and geese stop off here to rest every year in season, a sight to behold.

In the last few decades, the lake has become very 'old', a phenomenon caused by poor water-level control and the draining of huge amounts of fertilisers and other chemical and organic substances into the lake from the surrounding fields. Plans to establish a biosphere reserve in the lake have been discussed, which would be a step in the right direction to save the area's ecosystem and birdlife.

This precarious walkway gives you a good view of Lake Zuvintas

# Spa Towns

A popular destination for those seeking to improve their health or wishing to rejuvenate mind, body or spirit, Lithuania has enjoyed a great spa tradition for centuries. While many towns in the country offer spa treatments, the towns of Druskininkai and Bristonas are the most popular of the spa resorts. Famous for their mineral springs, Druskininkai and Bristonas have the added attraction of being set in picturesque surroundings. Palanga is another well-known retreat destination out of season – it is a very busy resort in summer.

Druskininkai, in the south of Lithuania, is the biggest and oldest health resort in the country (see also pp68–72). The local mud and mineral springs here are well known for their curative powers. Additionally, the town's location, 90m above sea level on the

right bank of the River Nemunas and surrounded by pine forests, ensures that the air in this resort is always clean and fresh. The healing properties of Druskininkai's mineral-water springs were first observed in the early 18th century. Throughout the 19th and 20th centuries, many wooden villas and small sanatoria were built, most of them specialising in mud and climate therapies. Heart, digestion and nervous diseases are only a few of the ailments treated here. The local mineral water is central to the treatments with patients drinking mineral water, undergoing mineral water-bath treatments, and taking mineral water inhalations. Rapid development in recent years has seen many high-standard facilities opening up in this area. Druskininkai's remarkably attractive and diverse surroundings make it an ideal town for walking and cycling around, for those who would like to combine their health stint with these gentle activities.

The other highly popular health resort is Bristonas, located 80km from Vilnius and 7km southeast of Prienai on the bend of the River Nemunas. The resort recently celebrated its 155th anniversary. When Druskininkai was annexed by Poland, Bristonas' popularity among Lithuanians as well as people from other nations rose quickly. Mineral water is the focal point of treatments here as well. Drinking, bathing and inhalations are included in the treatment of patients

with digestive disorders, blood circulation problems, kidney and respiratory diseases. The sanatoriums in Bristonas are open all year round. The town itself is beautiful, containing a museum of local teachings, a rowing station, as well as a tourist centre. Bristonas' Jazz Festival, held in early spring, attracts big crowds.

Neringa and Palanga in the west are also popular resorts (*see also pp102–103 & pp94–5*). Palanga is a climatic and mud-therapy resort with beaches by the Baltic Sea. However, it is very busy from June to August, making it a more relaxing place to visit off-season. Neringa is a bit quieter than Palanga. 'Neringa' is a German word for a long, narrow, strip of sand, and that is exactly what the town is. The most

popular sanatorium is Ąžuolynas, in the township of Juodkrantė.

Another spa resort is the expensive and elegant Le Méridien Villon near Vilnius. Spread over 154ha of natural beauty, the resort is surrounded by fabulous birch forests, beautiful lakes and scenic countryside. Its spa, called Oasis, focuses on the benefits of aromatherapy and physiotherapy, with treatments that revive, rejuvenate and restore the skin. This is a fairly exclusive resort, and you may definitely expect to experience high standards of service and treatment.

Facing page: Having taken the waters, spa visitors enjoy the peaceful surroundings
Above: International flags flutter at the entrance to one of Druskininkai's spas

*'Sculpture during this time was the strongest part of art in the Baltics. We were the best ones. Lithuanians just had the blood for sculpting.'*

**VYSNIAUSKA**

Located 130km southwest of Vilnius, on the road leading to the spa town of Druskininkai, is a unique sculpture park called Grutas Park. Spread over a 20ha area, the park is home to Soviet statues that were taken down from various sites when Lithuania re-established its independence in 1989, and contains 86 works by 46 different sculptors.

From 1989 to 1991, during the restoration of independence of the Baltic states, the fate of the Soviet statues was uncertain. Many were dismantled and piled into storehouses and backyards, while others were completely destroyed with dynamite in neighbouring republics.

Viliumas Malinauskas, a local mushroom farmer and entrepreneur, put forward a proposal to the Ministry of Culture – that these dismantled sculptures from the Soviet period be displayed in an exhibition. In 1998, his proposal was accepted, and preparatory work began in early 1999. Many of the statues had to be repaired – some of the works still bear marks of damage inflicted during the rebellion, such as blue and red paint, and the occasional fissure or dent.

There was much controversy over the opening of the park. Many Lithuanians strongly objected to the exhibition of these sculptures and other ideological relics. For those who had lost their loved ones during the oppressive regime or had suffered in other ways, the idea of having such an exposition, along theme-park lines, seemed like a travesty. Arguments in favour of it included the importance of this new tourist sight for southern Lithuania, and the fact that the park would not be a glorification of the former oppressors but rather the opposite. Grutas Park was officially opened on 1 April, 2001 – significantly known in Lithuania as the Day of Liars.

The stated aim of the museum-cum-park is to change the ideological purport of these huge sculptures by the way they are exhibited. Rather than glorifying the Soviet regime,

which was the original purpose of these statues, this park highlights the negative content of Soviet ideology and how it impacted the value system of this country.

The sculptures on display include Lenin, Stalin, Angarietis, Kapsukas, Dzerzhinsky, members of the Youth Communist League, soldiers, writers, workers and other Soviet heroes. The display symbolises the cruelty and absurdity of the Soviet regime. The order in which the monuments are displayed reflects the weight of the role that these people took in the organisation and implementation of terror, and in the annihilation of the sovereignty of Lithuania. Barbed wire fencing, watchtowers, replicas of cattle trucks such as were used to deport people – all these create the impression of a Siberian concentration camp in the middle of a Lithuanian forest.

## GRUTAS PARKAS

A wooden structure built in the style of houses of the 1940s and 50s, the park's information centre is a museum in itself, providing information on Soviet propaganda and the manipulative methods they used, giving a comprehensive picture of the genocide of the Lithuanian nation. You can also buy Soviet souvenirs here and sample Soviet-style food in the cafés and restaurants. *Grutas, 66441 Druskininkai. Tel: (370 313) 555 11; email: info@grutoparkas.lt. Open: daily winter 9am–5pm; summer 9am–8pm. Admission charge.*

Facing page: A history of the sculptures and the park in pictures lines the fence by the entrance
Above: The setting for the sculptures is gentle and peaceful, often in contrast to the ideas associated with the sculptures themselves

# Drive: Druskininkai to Alytus via Zuvintas Strict State Reserve

This drive is a purely scenic one, including a visit to the Zuvintas bird reserve and culminating in the winery town of Alytus. The roads are generally good in this part of the country and the scenery is mainly rural with rolling farmlands, small farmsteads and the industrious farmers going about their tasks.

*Time: 3½ hours.*

*Distance: 95km.*

Whole families venture out to their fields on Sundays to pick potatoes in season and to collect mushrooms. Horses and carts are still used in these areas on the farms, and occasionally a

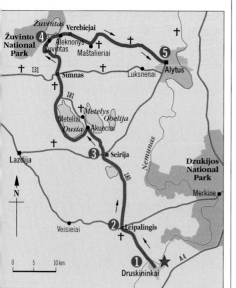

very old-fashioned tractor. This is not an area of great wealth but the farms are all well-kept and the surroundings are beautiful. You will notice white posts lining both sides of the road in this as in other areas of Lithuania. These are road markers for when the snow has set in to keep the driver from straying off the road into deep drifts.

## 1 Druskininkai

This lovely town makes for a good start to the drive (*see pp68–72*).

*Leave Druskininkai heading northwest on the 180, the road to Leipalingis.*

## 2 Leipalingis

*At Leipalingis follow the 180 in the direction of Seirija.*

## 3 Seirija

Just before Seirija, there is a small, pretty lake on the left-hand side of the road.

*At Seirija take the 181 north towards Simnas.*

To reach Zuvintas by a more scenic route, a few kilometres before Simnas, soon after a tiny village called Akuociai, there is a turning off to the left which will bring you to one of the two lakes that flank this stretch of road although they are only visible occasionally through the trees.

### 4 Zuvintas

*Back on the road continue into Simnas and head out of the town on the 181. A few kilometres after Simnas turn off the main road towards Zuvintas and you will see the signs for the reserve. You can see the marshy wetland and the lake in the distance when you take the turn off.*

There is a centre here with a tall statue of a crane on the grass in front of it. Walk down to the lake to its left and you come across a slatted wooden walkway out into the water. It is quite decrepit, so proceed with caution.

The views from here across the comparatively deeper part of the lake are lovely on a sunny day. Take a pair of binoculars if you want to do some birdwatching.

### 5 Alytus

*Continue on and the road will rejoin the 181 at Aleknoys, and shortly afterwards you will reach the village of Verebiejai. Take a right turn here and follow the road to Alytus.*

Clear road signs make travelling around Lithuania relatively simple

Laisvės Alėja, pedestrianised and lined with trees, stretches for 1.6km

## Kaunas

Kaunas was the capital of Lithuania for a period after the First World War and retains a stately charm in both its Old and New Town areas. Kaunas is Lithuania's second largest city in terms of population with around 380,000 inhabitants. It is an attractive place to spend a couple of days or to use as a base while exploring the southern part of the country. There are lots of things to see and do here. The Old Town is full of historic buildings and is a very attractive place to wander around. The New Town, built in the 19th century and linked to the Old Town at its eastern end, is no less interesting and contains the majority of the museums.

There is a very different atmosphere in the two parts of town: the Old Town is quieter and predominantly medieval in appearance – it is more a place of reverence than fun. By contrast the New Town, bisected by Laisvės Alėja (Freedom Avenue), is modern and vibrant. The history in this part of the city is about the 20th century struggles for independence and this is reflected in many of the buildings and told through the many museums. It is at this end of the city that most of the hotel and

> **Kaunas Tourist Information Centre**
> *Laisvės Alėja 36. Tel: (370 37) 323 436.*
> *turizmas@takas.lt. www.visit.kaunas.lt.*
> *Open: Sept–May Mon–Fri 9am–6pm, Sat*
> *9am–3pm; June–Aug Mon–Fri 9am–6pm,*
> *Sat 9am–1pm, Sun 2–6pm.*

restaurant development is taking place and offers the visitor a wide choice. However, there are some very special restaurants in the Old Town and a few hotels. For those looking for a quiet location this is probably the best choice.

Kaunas's geographical location on the confluence of the Neris and Nemunas rivers made it a place of extreme strategic importance in medieval times. As such, it was constantly under attack in the 14th century from the Crusaders, who were terrorising Lithuania. The fortress in Kaunas was successfully breached by the Teutonic Order in 1361; it was at this point that the town first appeared in the Chronicles. It had a period of prosperity and commercial importance after Lithuania's triumph at the Battle of Grunwald, as it was then able to use its excellent strategic location for promoting trade and business rather than for military defence purposes. Records from the 15th and 16th centuries show continued prosperity and consolidation of its position as a vital commercial centre. However, decay began to take hold of the city at the end of the 18th century and the ensuing century of Russian rule kept it very much behind Vilnius, which had managed to negotiate a certain amount of cultural autonomy from the Russian regime.

When Lithuania established its independent statehood after the conflict with Poland between the World Wars, Kaunas became the interim capital. With this new identity, it began to flourish. By the beginning of the 1930s, the city was reinventing itself as a capital with elegant architecture and a burgeoning cultural life. Kaunas became, and still is today, an important centre of learning and culture. It currently boasts seven professional theatres, the Philharmonic Hall, numerous museums, a thriving

The eternal flame lights up the Peace Memorial in Kaunas

The impressive Church of St Michael the Archangel

and well-respected university, and many other seats of learning and study.

The Old Town (*see Old Town Walk pp86–7*) is linked to the New Town area by Vilniaus gatvė, a delightful newly cobbled and restored street.

**A Zmuidzinavicius Art Museum**

Established in 1966, in the house of the artist Antanas Zmuidzinavicius (1876–1966), this museum houses major works of the artist as well as his personal collection of artefacts which he gifted to the Lithuanian government. The artist was a prolific collector of Lithuanian art, historic and ethnographic objects and folk artefacts. It is also known as the Devil's Museum as it exhibits a collection of over 2000 devil sculptures from all over the world (including those of Hitler and Stalin depicted as devils, doing the dance of death over a playground littered with human bones). *Putvinskio 64. Tel: (370 37) 221 587. Open: Tue–Sun 11am– 5pm. Closed: last Tue of every month. Admission charge.*

## Church of St Michael the Archangel

This huge neo-Byzantine church was built between 1891–93 for Orthodox worship, but finally became a Roman Catholic Church in 1990. It is also known as soboras after the Russian word '*sobor*' (cathedral). Designed and constructed by Russian architects it was built for the Kaunas Military Garrison. Later it was converted into an art gallery during the soviet period and reopened as a place of worship in the early nineties.
*Nepriklausomybes aikštė 14.*

*Man* by Petras Mazūras stands at the entrance to the Mykolas Žilinskas Art Museum

## Freedom Monument

Around the corner to the north of Laisvės Alėja, K Donelacio gatvė runs parallel to it and opening off it to the north is Vienybes alkste. Here in a large open space is the Freedom Monument. This symbol of Lithuanian statehood first appeared in the 1920s but was removed by the Stalinist regime. It was rebuilt in 1989 and is an impressive array of statues leading to an eternal flame.

## Laisvės Alėja

Vilniaus gatvė intersects the main pedestrian street, Laisvės Alėja, in the newer part of the city. Also called Freedom Avenue, the latter is 1.6km long, straight, tree-lined and wide. Containing the city's smartest hotels and trendiest restaurants and bars, the pedestrianised street is also a paradise for shoppers. It is a popular meeting-place for Kaunas's young people who spend hours walking up and down, stopping at the occasional café or just chatting in groups.

## Mykolas Žilinskas Art Museum

Just across the square from the Church of St Michael the Archangel is the fine Mykolas Žilinskas Art Museum. On the ground floor is an exhibition of decorative art; paintings and sculptures are displayed on the two upper floors. Outside the museum you cannot fail to see Petras Mazūras's sculpture of a nude man, which caused a certain amount of outrage when it was installed in 1990.
*Nepriklausomybes aikštė 12.
Open: Tue–Sun 11am–5pm. Closed: last Tue of every month. Admission charge.*

Children playing outside the War Museum

## Vytautas the Great War Museum

Huge bronze lions guard the entrance of Vytautas the Great War Museum which was founded in the 1920s to honour the history of Lithuania. One of the most well-known exhibits is the wreck of the Lithuanian aviators, Darius and Girėnas's aeroplane *Lituanica*. These two national heroes, Steponas Darius and Stasys Girėnas were born in Lithuania but lived in the United States. Their bravery and daring led them to be embraced into Lithuanian historical culture. They plunged to their deaths in 1933 as they were attempting to break the world record for the longest transatlantic flight. There is a 25m-high bronze memorial statue to the pair in Sporto and Perkūno which was erected in the late 1990s.
*64 Donelaicio St. Tel: (370 37) 320 765, (370 37) 422 146; Open: Wed–Sun 10am–5pm. Closed: last Thur of every month. Admission charge.*

## Kėdainiai

Its title as pickled gherkin or cucumber capital of the Baltics gives no indication of the charm and attractiveness of this provincial town. Located about half an hour from Kaunas and an hour and a half from Vilnius it is a very convenient stop-off on a tour of the area as well as an extremely pleasant destination in its own right. This market town is set on the banks of the River Nevezis and has an attractive and well preserved old town with a fine main square. In the early 16th century it was owned by the grand Protestant Radvila family who tried to establish the town as an intellectual and cultural centre. Any remaining signs of Protestant culture date from this period. The variety of churches and two synagogues are evidence of the tolerance and inclusiveness that Kėdainiai has shown; embracing Jewish, Russian Orthodox, Arian and Catholic communities over the centuries.

The Old Town is the most attractive part of town and is reached by turning off the main Basanaviciaus gatvė into Didžioji. You will find the Tourist Office in this street and this makes a good starting point. Didžioji Rinka and Senoji Rinka, Great Market and Old Market respectively are two substantial squares containing the main concentration of interesting buildings and the two synagogues.

## Kėdainiai Regional Museum

The museum is housed in an attractive 18th century former Carmelite convent. Unsurprisingly there are a substantial number of exhibits relating to the town's most renowned resident Duke Jonušas Radvila (1612–1655) including a number of portraits of different members of his illustrious family. It is also interesting to trace the development of the town which is interestingly presented through the use of models and pictures. One exhibit you must not miss if only to marvel at the grossness of it, is the room of 19th-century furniture made out of antlers.

*Didžioji 19. Tel: (370 347) 536 85; email: muziejus@kedainiai.omnitel.net. Open: Tue–Sat 9am–5pm. Admission charge.*

**Reformatu baznycia (The Evangelical Reform Church)**

This is one of the town's main landmarks and is of interest both as a fine example of this type of austere Protestant architecture but more importantly, in local history terms, for the mausoleum of the Radvila Dukes. Considered the most notable royal grave in Lithuania, the mausoleum is in the basement of this church underneath the main altar. The remains of Jonušas, his grandfather Kristupas 'the Thunderer' and four of Jonušas's siblings are laid out in wonderfully ornate Baroque coffins of varying sizes. The largest and grandest belongs to Jonušas and the four small coffins on little brass legs belong to his infant siblings.

*Senoji 1. Contact the Tourist Office to organise a visit to either the church and/or the mausoleum. Admission charge.*

The existence of a once substantial Jewish community in Kėdainiai is evidenced by the two remaining synagogues in the Old Town. They first came to the town in the 15th century but were banished at the end of that century by Archduke Alexander. It wasn't until the mid 17th century that the Jewish community was properly established and then, as licensors for the production of beer and spirits, they became the hostelry owners and the social and economic backbone of the population. Since the devastation of the Jewish community here during the Second World War little of their cultural heritage remains except for the two synagogues: the larger of the two now operates as an art school and the smaller is the Daugiakultūris centras (Kėdainiai Multicultural Centre) which is run as an art gallery. Definitely worth a visit, exhibitions of contemporary art, sculpture and photography are held throughout the year.

*Senoji Rinka. Open: Tue–Sat 10am–5pm. Tel: ( 370 347) 270 10 52. Admission charge.*

Look out for the Kėdainiai Minaret on the north side of the River Dotnuvėlė. It is a folly built in the 1880s by Count von Totleben who lived nearby. The Minaret is definitely an oddity and has become a bit dilapidated but the whole setting in attractive parkland close to the river makes it an enjoyable place to visit.

**Kėdainiai Tourist Information**
**Tourist Office:** *Didžioji 1. Tel: (370 347) 603 63. Open: Mon–Sat 8am–5pm.*
*email: kedainiai@centras.lt, www.kedainiai.lt*
**Police:** *Mickevičiaus 23. Tel: (370 347) 542 13.*
**Hospital:** *Budrio 5. Tel: (370 347) 670 90.*
**Train Station:** *Dariaus ir Giréno 3. Tel: (370 347) 523 33. Open: 6–11.30am, 4–9pm.*
**Bus Station:** *Basanavičiaus 93. Tel: (370 347) 603 33. Open: 5am–10.45pm.*

# Walk: Kaunas Old Town

Boasting majestic buildings and fine stonework, the Old
Town of Kaunas is a wonderful place to wander around to
fully appreciate its many charms. This walk begins in the
13th-century main street, Vilniaus gatvė, and takes you
around the main sights of the Old Town up to the Castle,
down to the river and back to the main street.

*Time: Allow 2–3 hours.*

*Distance: 2.5km.*

*Begin the walk at Dievo Kuno
Dominikonų Baznycia ir Vienuolynas
(Dominican Church and Monastery of the
Lord's Body). Walk down Vilniaus gatvė.*

## 1 Šv Apaštalų Petro ir Pauliaus Arkikatedra-Bazilika (Arch-Cathedral Basilica of Apostles St Peter and St Paul)

This cathedral is the largest Gothic
church in Lithuania, as well as the only
Gothic church with a basilica floor plan.
(Gothic churches usually have a cross-
shaped floor plan.) Another interesting

feature in the cathedral for literature-
minded visitors is the tomb of the priest
and poet Maironis in the south wall – he
has been described as one of the
founders of the Lithuanian modern
poetry movement.

*Turn right up M Valančiaus gatvė and
take the second left into Pilies gatvė.
Continue down Pilies gatvė across A
Jaksto gatvė to reach Kauno Pilis.*

## 2 Kauno Pilis (Kaunas Castle)

The oldest building in the city, it had
been in existence years before it was

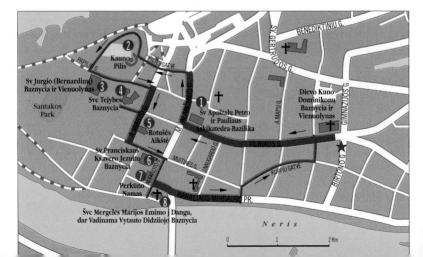

first chronicled in 1361. Its strategic position on a peninsula-like piece of land flanked by the confluence of the Neris and Nemunas rivers led to it being constantly under attack during the 14th century.
*Walk around the castle and into the park, coming back onto Papilio gatvė.*

### 3  Šv Jurgio (Bernardinų) Baznycia ir Vienuolynas (St George's (or Bernardine) Church and Monastery)
This friary was built for the Bernardine Order in Gothic style in the 15th century. Its condition deteriorated greatly during the Soviet regime and it is currently under restoration.
*Continue along Papilio gatvė, turning right into A Jaksto and right again when you reach the square.*

### 4  Švc Tejybes Baznycia (St Trinity Church)
Now used as a dance studio, this structure features an interesting mixture of Renaissance and Gothic architectural elements which are now evident only on the exterior.
*Walk back into the main square.*

### 5  Rotušės Aikštė (Town Hall)
Dating from the mid-16th century, this striking edifice is predominantly late baroque in style, with touches of early Classicism and Gothic architecture. It has been utilised for a variety of different activities over the centuries, but is best remembered as a Soviet wedding palace, possibly giving it the nickname White Swan, by which it is often referred to.
*Turn left down Mutines gatvė.*

### 6  Šv Pranciskaus Ksavero Jezuitu Baznycia (St Francis Xavier Jesuit Church)
Built in 1666, the church has had a rather chequered history, starting with being burnt down even as it was being built. In 1825, it was converted to Russian Orthodox use and renamed after Alexander Nevsky and raised to cathedral status in 1843. It was returned briefly to the Jesuits after the First World War, but taken back shortly afterwards and used as a school during the Soviet era. It has been back in service since 1990.
*Turn right down Aleksoto gatvė.*

### 7  Perkūno Namas (Perkunas (Thunder) House)
Built at the end of the 15th century, this exceptional church is one of the finest examples of late Gothic architecture. Under the control of Jesuits and tradesmen at various points in its history, it is currently a venue for art classes.
*Walk on down Aleksoto gatvė till you reach the river.*

### 8  Švc Mergeles Marijos Emimo j Dangu, dar Vadinama Vytauto Didžiiojo Baznycia (Church of St Mary the Virgin's Ascension to Heaven)
Also called the Church of Vytautas the Great, it claims a dramatic position right on the riverbank. However, the church itself looks a bit neglected and grim.
*Walk along the river on Karaliaus Mindaugo Prospektas. Turn left up M Daukšos and right into Kurpiu gatvė, continue along here and turn left at Palangos gatvė and take the first right into Vilniaus gatvė.*

# The Baltic Coast

Lithuania's Baltic Coast offers a variety of attractions for visitors and is the most tourist-oriented area of the country. The *pièce de résistance* is Kuršių Nerija, known as the Curonian Spit. One of the country's designated national parks, it was also recognised by UNESCO in 2000 as a World Heritage Landscape. Stretching 97km in length and only 4km wide, much less in places, this thin spit of land consists mainly of forests and dunes and protects a huge inland body of water, the Curonian Lagoon, and the mainland from the rigours of the Baltic Sea.

Dunes of soft sand line Lithuania's Baltic Coast

The Spit is accessible from the mainland by ferries which run from ports on the outskirts of Klaipėda, Lithuania's third city. About 30km north of Klaipėda is the country's main seaside resort of Palanga, which is a lively and attractive place immensely popular both with Lithuanians and tourists.

Sunset over the Baltic Sea

# The Baltic Coast

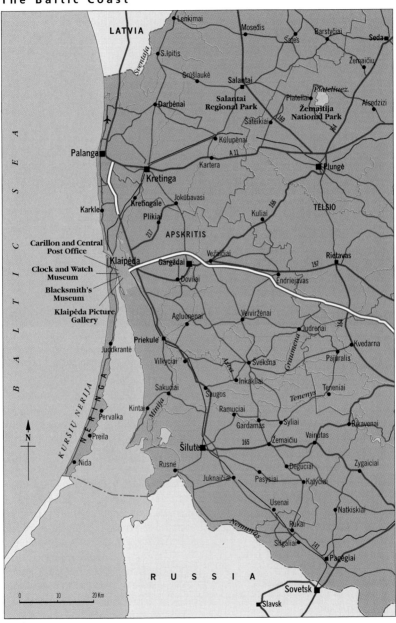

German influence in the architecture is evident in these buildings in Klaipėda

## Klaipėda

With over 203,000 inhabitants, Klaipėda is the third largest city in the country population-wise. In terms of commercial and strategic importance and cosmopolitan appeal, Klaipėda could be rated as Lithuania's second city rather than Kaunas (*see pp80–4*), which has a larger population.

Built around Lithuania's only port, Klaipėda and its two satellite holiday resorts, Nida to the south and Palanga to the north, are well on their way to becoming the Baltic Riviera. In summer,

**Klaipėda Tourist Information**
*Turgaus gatvė 7, LT-91247. Tel: (370 46) 412 186. www.klaipeda.lt*

the city itelf is usually not the main attraction, with most tourists heading towards the beach resorts nearby. But with its many museums, monuments, galleries and historic buildings, it has plenty to occupy those interested in some sightseeing and culture, at any time of the year.

Klaipėda has been part of Lithuania only since 1923 when it was seized by the inter-war republic. For most of its previous life it had existed as the German city of Memel, and was the easternmost outpost of the Second Reich. Once you are aware of its history, the architecture prevalent in the older part of town begins to make sense. There are some lovely buildings here, but they are surprisingly different from the architecture in the other Lithuanian cities. The rest of the city has changed completely as has the population, which now consists mainly of Lithuanians and a sizeable Russian population, who settled here after the Second World War. The German population has all but disappeared.

Like Vilinus and Kaunas, Klaipėda too has two distinct parts. The Old Town, where most of the museums are located, is to the south of the River Dane, which bisects the city; the New Town spreads out from its northern bank.

## Kalvystės Muziejus (Blacksmith's Museum)

A few minutes' walk from Theatre Square, the focal point of the Old Town, leads visitors to this excellent interactive museum. Watch the action at a real working forge manned by hardworking blacksmiths. Also included are a number of interesting metalwork exhibits such as church weather vanes and metal crosses.
*Saltkalviu 2. Tel: (370 46) 410 526. Open: Tue–Sat 10am–5.30pm. Admission charge.*

## Carillon and Central Post Office

Don't miss this edifice on the New Town's main street, Liepu gatvė. An outstanding example of Gothic architecture, this red brick mansion was designed by the German architect H Schode in 1893 and is a beautiful building both inside and out. Alongside is a 44m bell tower that houses the largest musical instrument in the country. Built in Apolde in Germany, the immense 48-bell carillon is rung at noon on weekends, and concerts are also organised at times.

## Laiktodsiu Muziejus (Clock and Watch Museum)

An unusual and interesting museum at Liepu gatvė 12 is Laiktodsiu Muziejus (Clock and Watch Museum). It contains timepieces from the earliest days – candles only – to the present. Some simple, some incredibly complex and some exuberantly flamboyant 17th and 18th century examples. It is an extremely enjoyable experience.
*Liepu gatvė 12. Tel: (370 46) 410 413. Open: Tue–Sat noon–5.30pm, Sun noon–4.30pm. Admission charge.*

## Mažosios Lietuvos Istorijos Muziejus (History Museum of Lithuania Minor)

It is worth stopping off at this Old Town attraction to get some sense of the history of the city and surrounding area. The collection is eclectic and interesting and just being inside the building is an experience in itself – the interior resembles the inside of a wooden sailing ship.
*Didžioji Vandens 6. Tel: (370 46) 410 523. Open: Tue–Sat 10am–5.30pm. Closed: Wed–Sun. Admission charge.*

### Annchen von Tarau (Taravos Anike)

The statue of the girl standing with her back to the Drama Theatre was dedicated to the German poet Simon Dach (1605–59), who wrote a famous folk song about the girl. The story of the girl is a bit of a mystery. All that is known is that the statue of her disappeared some time during the Second World War. She was either abducted by the Soviets or the Nazis, who were apparently upset that her back was turned towards Hitler when he addressed the masses from the theatre's balcony. The current statue is a replica made in 1989 from photographs of the original.

Annchen von Tarau and the Drama Theatre

**P. Domšaitis' Gallery
(Klaipėda Picture Gallery)**
If you are interested in Lithuanian art,
visit the gallery on Liepu gatvė. There is
a large collection of Lithuanian
paintings from the Impressionist period
to present day as well as an intriguing
open-air sculpture gallery.
*Liepu gatvė 33. Tel: (370 46) 300 164.
Open: Tue–Sat noon–6pm, Sun
noon–5pm. Admission charge.*

**Old Buildings**
Interesting and picturesque old
buildings in the Old Town area include
the **Old Post Office** (*No.13 on Aukštoji,
just off Didžioji*), and the half-timbered
former fish warehouse that now
functions as the **Exhibition Hall**

(*Aukštoji 3*). One of Klaipėda's most
outstanding examples of half-timbering
is **Elephant House** (*Darzu 10*), a short
walk from the Exhibition Hall.

**Teatro aikštė (Theatre Square)**
The centre of the Old Town, Theatre
Square is dominated by the 19th-
century Drama Theatre. This has been
the venue for many significant cultural
and political events – Hitler announced
Klaipėda's re-incorporation into
Germany from the building's exterior
balcony and Wagner performed here as
a visiting conductor.
　The statue of Annchen von Tarau
erected in 1912 in front of the Drama
Theatre is dedicated to the German poet
Simon Dach (1605–59).

Notice some of the interesting features on Klaipėda's older buildings

**Mažvydo Skulptūrų Parkas
(Mažvydas Sculpture Park)**
One of Klaipėda's most famous sons was
the 16th century scholar, priest and
publicist Martynas Mažvydas. His book
of Catechisms is renowned as the first
book to be published in Lithuania in
1547. There are two memorials to him
in Klaipėda: the Mažvydo Skulptūrų
Parkas (Mažvydas Sculpture Park)
situated in the New Town between Liepu
gatvė and S Daukanto gatvė, and the
Martyno Mažvydo Paminklas
(Memorial to Martynas Mažvydas) by
R Midvikis erected in 1997 in
Lietuvininkų aikštė to the northwest of
the park. The sculpture park is set on
what was until 1977 the city's main
cemetery. In 1977 the Soviets ordered
the destruction of the cemetery and the
sculpture park gradually evolved. There
are a number of representations of

the great man as well as an assortment
of other unusual and sometimes
startling pieces.
*O/P-3, Between Liepø and Daukanto.*

When you've had enough of sightseeing and fancy a break, head north out
of Klapėida either on foot, bicycle or bus
towards Palanga and you soon reach the
beautiful sandy beaches of Melnragė
and then a bit further on to Giruliai.
There are many outdoor restaurants,
cafés and bars lining the beaches as well
as a smattering of water sports. Just to
the south of the city, Smiltyne is a
popular beach area reached by a short
ferry ride from Klaipėda.

**Palanga**
This is the country's premier seaside
and health resort, combining the bustle
of a resort with places to get away

The pier stretching out into roughish seas under an overcast sky

Ready for action on Palanga's long sandy beach

from it all. There are long, pale sandy beaches backed by dunes, excellent swimming, a large botanical garden and a vibrant town with all the modern facilities.

Palanga's resident population of around 20,000 swells to over 100,000 between June and August, when Lithuanians from all over the country and tourists from neighbouring countries descend upon it in droves. It is hard to imagine now that the town was once a fishing village and later Lithuania's main port from the 15th to 17th centuries. Its popularity as a resort and health spa grew in the 19th century when Count Felix Tiškevičius bought a large estate on the outskirts of the town and built a huge mansion and park. This inspired others to set up guesthouses and by the beginning of the 20th century, Palanga had become a fashionable health resort, favoured by the aristocracy of Lithuania, Poland and Russia.

**IMPORTANT TOURIST INFORMATION**
**Currency exchanges:**
*Taikos av. 28. Tel: (370 46) 41821.*
*Open: daily 8am–10pm.*
*Vytauto gatvė 19. Tel: (370 46) 411 996.*
*Open: daily 9am–8pm.*
**Klaipėda cruise ship terminal:** *Pilies gatvė 4. Tel: (370 46) 490 990. www.ports.lt*
**Klaipėda State Seaport Administration:** *J.Janonio gatvė 24. Tel: (370 46) 499 979. www.portofklaipeda.lt*
**International ferry terminal:** *Perkelos gatvė 10. Tel: (370 46) 395 050.*
*www.lisco.lt or www.scandlines.de*
**Klaipėda railway station:** *Priestoties gatvė 1. Tel: (370 46) 313 677. www.litrail.lt*
**Klaipėda bus station:** *Butku Juzes gatvė 9. www.klap.lt*
**Palanga/Klaipėda international airport:** *Liepojos pl.1, Palanga. Tel: (370 46) 352 020. www.palanga-airport.lt*
**Pharmacy:** *Taikos pr. 81. Tel: (370 46) 341 298. Open: 24hrs.*
**Yacht port:** *Pilies gatvė 4. Tel: (370 46) 490 990. www.ports.lt*
**For further information contact the Klaipėda Tourist and Cultural Information Centre:** *Turgaus gatvė 7, LT-91247, Klaipėda. www.klaipeda.lt*

# Walk: Palanga

The whole resort area is relatively compact and makes a pleasant stroll. This route does not include wandering among the residential houses in the resort but this could be a pleasant diversion – in fact, several variations from this route are possible. Most of the hotels and B&Bs are scattered around the otherwise residential streets between the main street of the town and the sea.

*Time: Allow about 2 hours, depending on how long you want to spend in the Botanical Park.*

*Distance: 3km.*

*Start the walk at the information centre at the intersection of Kretingos gatvė and Vytauto gatvė (on the main street near the supermarket Maxima and bus station).*

## 1 Neo-Gothic Catholic Church

The red brick neo-Gothic Catholic Church on the right-hand side is a striking edifice built in 1909, and is the venue for the St Rokas Festival at the end of August.

*Continue along Vytauto gatvė until you reach the Botanical Park.*

## 2 Palanga Botanical Park

Designed by the renowned French landscape architect Édouard André (1867–1942), this park was commissioned by Count Felix Tiškevičius in 1897. Covering an area of 100ha, this beautiful park is considered one of the best preserved parks on the coast. It covers a large swathe of the southern end of the resort town, and is a wonderfully cool place to wander in during the heat of the summer.

## 3 Statue of the Three Sisters

You will see this statue just inside the entrance to the Botanical Park.

*Cut across the Park and you will come to the Amber Museum.*

## 4 Amber Museum

The fine neo-classical mansion that houses this excellent museum was built at the end of the 19th century

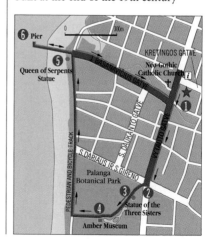

for Count Tiškevičius' family. The museum details a clear and interesting history of this semi-precious stone, and displays hundreds of interesting pieces of amber. Concerts and recitals are held here throughout the year.

*Walk on through the park till you reach the beach and a pedestrian and bicycle track. Turn right and walk back towards the town centre. Alternatively, you can walk along the beach by heading straight across the track and over the dunes. Then turn right onto the beach. If you are walking down the track, you will come out into an open paved square, where you can see the Queen of Serpents statue.*

### 5 Queen of Serpents Statue

Sculpted by Robertas Antinis, this is one of the most well-known statues in the country (*see pp98–9*).

*Head for the beach over the dunes and you come to Palanga's pier.*

### 6 Pier

This pier has had many incarnations. Built originally as a landing stage for ships, it has been washed away several times by storms. The present structure is a celebrated feature of the resort of Palanga and a focal point for meeting and strolling.

*Head back over the dunes and you find yourself at the beginning of one of the resort's main boulevards.*

### 7 Basanavicius Gatvė

The most popular street in Palanga, this has recently been reconstructed and smartened up. It is a favourite haunt for both young and old, and serves as the resort's main promenade. Lined with cafés, bars, restaurants and some shops, this is the street where most of the action in Palanga occurs.

*Walk down to the end of Basanavicius gatvė to where it intersects Vytauto gatvė, the road where the walk began. The walk northwards down this attractive and wide main street is interesting, as this stretch features the resort's most sophisticated shopping opportunities.*

**Amber Museum** *Open: Tue–Sun 10am–6pm. Admission charge.*

Amber Museum

A long time ago, according to the best-known Lithuanian legend, lived an old man and his wife, who had 12 sons and three daughters. One hot summer's day, the three sisters decided to go for a dip in a lake to cool off. After their swim, they climbed back onto the riverbank to put on their clothes. To her distress, Egle, the youngest of the three girls, found a snake inside her blouse. The eldest sister attempted to scare off the snake by shaking the blouse and jumping on it, but to no avail. The snake turned to Egle and spoke in a man's voice, asking for her hand in marriage in return for not harming her or her sisters. Feeling she had no choice, Egle agreed through a mist of tears.

When the girls came back to their home, which they shared with their parents and 12 brothers, hundreds of snakes surrounded the house demanding that Egle return with them to the lake to fulfil her promise. Egle's father, who did not want to lose his youngest and most beautiful daughter, tried to trick the snakes by sending along different animals dressed as Egle. This did nothing but anger the serpents, who returned to the farm demanding the bride. Eventually Egle's father had no choice but to give up his daughter. Reluctantly, Egle left her home. To her surprise, she was greeted by a handsome prince who was waiting for her by the beach. The prince commented on how much he enjoyed watching her swim. Needless to say, Egle instantly fell in love with the prince and they were married, and soon had children. Egle was so happy that she forgot her homeland. They lived together happily in the lake for many years until fate took an unexpected and dark turn for them.

One day, Egle's three sons asked if they could meet their grandparents. It was only at this point that Egle remembered her old home and naturally she agreed to take them to visit her family. However, while visiting the family, Egle's daughter was tricked

by Egle's brothers into revealing how to call forth her father from the lake. The brothers took off to the lakeside with this information and called Egle's husband from the waters. When he swam up, the brothers chopped the serpent to pieces. They then returned to the farm and did not breathe a word of their deed to Egle. Nine days passed, and Egle returned to the lake to be united with her husband. When she called for him she was greeted by foam and blood, and she heard the voice of her beloved husband, telling her what her brothers had done. Heartbroken, Egle in utter despair turned herself and her children into trees.

There are two sculptures of Egle, Queen of Serpents, in Palanga, one near the northern end of the Botanical Gardens and the other, by Robertas Antinis, at the beach end of Basanavicius gatvė. A sculpture of the three sisters, by Z Pranaityte, is located on the sand dunes by the main entrance to Palanga beach.

Above: Egle shaking the serpent out of her shirt
Facing page: Another representation of the famous Lithuanian legend

Dunes and beach on the Curonian Spit

### Kuršių Nerija (The Curonian Spit)

A unique, quite wonderful piece of land, the Curonian Spit (also known as the Neringa National Park) is a thin peninsula of sand that is covered by forests and dunes, and protects the huge inland body of water called the Curonian Lagoon, as well as the mainland, from the rigours of the Baltic Sea. The spit covers a length of 97km, but only a stretch of 52km belongs to Lithuania; the remainder is Russian territory (the Kaliningrad enclave). Extending from the Semba Peninsula in the south to the Strait of Klaipėda in the north, it is 4km across at its widest point and at the narrowest point, the Baltic

Sea is separated from the Curonian Lagoon by only 400m.

The Curonian Spit was created more than 5,000 years ago by the waves and winds of the Baltic Sea. The spit's formation began when a barren strip of sand separated the Curonian Lagoon from the Baltic Sea. Over the passage of time, the sand gradually shifted eastwards and was deposited in the lagoon, thus forming the Curonian Spit. Its eastern shore is on the Curonian Lagoon, while the western shore of the peninsula is met by the Baltic Sea; therefore a sand dune that runs the length of the shoreline was artificially created to protect the spit from being washed into the sea. The Lithuanian authorities have set out strict guidelines in order to protect the spit and its native flora and fauna. Half of the territory on the Lithuanian end has been assigned to landscape reserves. One fifth is designated for recreational use.

The Lithuanian part of the spit can only be reached by ferry, while it is connected to land at the Russian end. Unfortunately, there is still plenty of red tape at the Russian border, preventing easy trips to this part of the spit.

There are two ferry services from Klaipėda to the spit, running at regular intervals. Numerous minibuses service the area, so it is not necessary to bring your own vehicle. However, having your own car gives you the freedom to explore at leisure. Once you arrive on the spit, if you haven't brought a vehicle, flag down any of the minibuses to get to the main beaches. The permit needed to travel to the municipality of Neringa is available for purchase when you arrive. No permit is required to visit the other beach towns such as Kopgalis or Smiltyne.

Around 72 per cent of the Curonian Spit is covered by forests. The fact that such a large forest cover of mostly conifers and grasslands is possible on the sandy soil of the spit is remarkable in itself. Several unusual species of flora are found here. Sand dunes occupy 12 per cent of the area. The spit's unique landscape of high and bare sand dunes alternating with forest cover harbours a variety of wildlife, especially birdlife. Its position makes it an important spot for studying routes taken by migratory birds.

From the top of the high sand dunes

The calm inshore waters of the Curonian Lagoon, Neringa

you get an unforgettable view – on one side are the rolling waves of the Baltic Sea and on the other, the waters of the Curonian Lagoon. Between these two bodies of water, a strip of sand stretches into the distance, with glades, sparse settlements, lighthouses and forests. The spit's unique features led UNESCO to designate it as a World Heritage Landscape in 2000.

### Neringa

The longest town in Lithuania at 50km, Neringa's population now stands at 2,700. It was formed in 1961 when the separate villages of Nida, Preila, Pervalka and Juodkrantė, strung along the Curonian Spit, were joined to form a single administrative unit called the town of Neringa.

There is plenty to do for even those not interested in swimming or sunbathing on the pristine beaches. The lagoon is a great place to fish, row or sail. Visitors can explore the forests, which are full of mushrooms and berries. Picking mushrooms is a national pastime and wherever you go in Lithuania in season, you are likely to see people out with bags and baskets scouring the ground for these tasty delicacies – the spit is a good place to do as the Lithuanians do. In the morning you can look on the beach for pieces of amber, as the sea sometimes washes handfuls of pieces ashore.

The forest plays a vital role in protecting the villages of Neringa from the shifting sands. The architecture of these seaside settlements on the Curonian Spit is interesting – nowhere else in Lithuania will you see so many

Neat, well-kept grounds stretch down to a walkway along the inner shoreline

colourfully decorated houses. Bright weather vanes stand out on the roofs of the houses along the Spit, now as since time immemorial, it is important for a fisherman to know which way the wind is blowing. The evening air in Neringa often smells of smoked fish. Fishing is not simply an occupation on the Curonian Spit, it is a way of life.

### Nida

The biggest settlement and the most popular destination on the spit is Nida. It can be a bit overcrowded in the peak season, attracting over 50,000 tourists per year, so unless you revel in the bustle, the best time to go is out of season. Nida is surrounded by pine groves, and is fabulous in winter when the lagoon freezes over. It is a good idea to go at that time if you are looking for some peace and quiet in lovely surroundings. However, there's plenty to do here for those so inclined. A host of museums await the culture aficionado.

Two aspects of this resort, and for some its main draw, are the dunes and the beach. Not far south of the village, approached from the village itself, is a path that leads to wooden steps that climb to the top of Parnidžio Kopa (Parnidis Dune). Fifty metres high, it is one of the largest dunes on the Curonian Spit, with great views from its summit. The beach, a fantastic stretch of pale sand, can be reached by walking westwards from here or from the village.

Over the years Nida has drawn holidaymakers from both inside and outside of Lithuania and remains a lively, cosmopolitan resort today. It is renowned for its brightly coloured,

thatched roofed, traditional fishermen's houses. Close to the main square down some of the small narrow streets you can see rows of these immaculately kept, brightly painted houses complete with picture-book gardens separated by picket fences. If you want to get an insight into the domestic life of the Curonian fishermen the place to go is the **Žvejo Etnografine Sodyba (Fishermen's Ethnographic Homestead)**.

This simple oblong wooded structure is done out as a reconstruction of a traditional fisherman's house. They were designed to accommodate a family at each end and the homestead is immaculately decorated to match its exterior.

*Nagliu 4. Open: May–Sept Tue–Sun 11am–7pm. Admission charge.*

To learn more about the fishermen's way of life a visit to the **Kuršių Nerijos Gyventoju Verslų Ekspozicija (Curonian Spit Livelihood Exhibition)** is a must. Scale models of the various types of fishing craft and other related conveyances can be examined and there are examples and information on the weather vanes that are peculiar to the fishing fleet of the Curonian Spit. You

---

**Boat Cruises on the Lagoon**

Many cruise companies offer one-day trips around the Curonian Lagoon. This is a beautiful way to view the natural wonder of the spit, a listed UNESCO World Heritage Site. The ships leave the Klaipėda cruise ships' terminal at 10am and do not return until 10.30pm. Your ship will stop at the settlements along Neringa, giving you time to explore each. It usually makes a three-hour stop in Nida, giving you a longer period of time to spend at this unique part of the spit. For more details see *www.jukunda.lt*

The Baltic Coast visible over the trees

can also learn about the practices and history of the trade from the photographs and commentary on display.

*Kuverto 2. Open: May–Sept Tue–Sun 11am–7pm. Admission charge.*
*www.neringosmuz@is.lt*

Thomas Mann, the renowned writer, visited here in 1929 and was so enamoured with the place that he decided to build his own summer house here. **Tomo Manno namelis (Thomas Mann's House)** is a completely charming thatched roofed cottage which has been converted into a museum dedicated to the writer and his family. It is really a museum for Mann enthusiasts and has photographs of his family, letters and editions of his books.

*17 Skruzdynes. Tel: (370 469) 522 60.*
*Email: mann@nida.omnitel.net*
*Open: May–Sept Tue–Sun 11am–5pm.*
*Admission charge.*

**Gintaro Galerija (Amber Gallery)**
This collection of unique objects was being built piece by piece in Juodkrantė and Nida for over 20 years. The biggest piece of amber weighs more than 3 kg. There are also other valuable pieces weighing 1.5 and 1kg. The gallery features amber in all its colours and forms as well as some unique pieces of restored antique jewellery and some created by Lithuanian artists.
*Pamario 20. Tel: (370 469) 525 73.*
*Open: Sept–May 10am–7pm, Jun–Aug 9am–9pm.*

## Catholic Church

This rather unusual and extremely modern church with a bright red roof quite dominates Nida's skyline. It also houses a small art gallery.
*Taikos 10. Open for service: daily 6pm, Sun noon. Tel: (370 469) 521 32.*

## Evangelical-Lutheran Church

Built in 1888, this redbrick church is renowned for its *kriskstai*, which are a way of marking and protecting the different graves. The shape and size of the *kriskstai* indicate the age and sex of the deceased.
*Pamario 43.*

## Neringa Historical Museum

Housed in a modern building near Hotel Hermann Blode the museum presents traditional trades of the inhabitants of the Curonian Spit, such as fishing and crow hunting. Also displayed is the equipment that went with these occupations such as fishing tackle and a range of model boats that were used, such as *kurėnas* (a small Curonian boat) and the nets that were used to trap crows. Other galleries contain discoveries from the New Stone Age found south of Nida and other features that illustrate Nida's history and give you a sense of the daily life of its people at the end of the 19th century. One section is dedicated to the noble family of the Froeses who had lived in Nida for several centuries. More info on: *www.neringainfo.lt*
*Pamario 53. Tel: (370 469) 511 62. Open: daily 10am–7pm; closed: Mon.*

One of the many folk art pieces on display in Neringa

# Drive: The Curonian Spit

This exhilarating and scenic drive, along the spectacular natural formation that is the Curonian Spit, takes in rustic villages, old woods, a refreshing seascape and even a number of interesting museums.

*Time: Allow for 3–4 hours.*
*Distance: 100km.*

*Catch the ferry from either of the ports in Klaipėda in the morning; boats leave at regular intervals. On arrival, head for the introductory pathway by the old woods of the Curonian Spit.*

## 1 Introductory Pathway

The pathway, which is 1.6km long, has stands that provide descriptions, pictures and drawings of the plants that grow in the area. It is a good introduction to the natural life of the spit. (There is another introductory pathway at the Nagliai Reserve, at the 31st km on the Nida–Smiltyne highway).

*Head south when finished here, towards Neringa. The permit to visit the town of Neringa can be bought from a kiosk at the entrance to the area.*

## 2 Juodkrantė

The first village Juodkrantė is 19km south of Klaipėda. It is the second biggest settlement on Neringa, after Nida. The beach was awarded a blue flag in 2004. Take some time to have a look around this quaint village. The main focus of the village is a promenade along

A typical Lithuanian sunset on the Curonian Spit

the lagoon with many points of tourist interest along the way. There are a few boats moored here, and generally it is a quiet and restful place. There is one small grocery shop and a number of houses sell smoked fish from their converted porches.

Stop at the Witches' Hill exposition of wooden outdoor sculptures. In 1979–80, folk artists congregated on Juodkrantė to create the 70-odd sculptures.

Another attraction of the area is one of Lithuania's oldest colonies of grey egrets and big cormorants just outside Juodkrantė.

### 3 Pervalka
This is the smallest of the settlements on Neringa. Bordered by a range of dunes to the west, it is 34km from Klaipėda. Stop by briefly if you wish to look around the small souvenir shops or buy some smoked fish.

### 4 Preila
Located on a bay between the capes of Preila and Ozku, 39km from Klaipėda, this settlement offers magnificent views of the lagoon. The dunes here are covered with grass and other foliage. The settlement is small but cosy, making it a good retreat destination.

### 5 Nida
The largest settlement on the spit is the town of Nida, the administrative centre of Neringa. The beach was awarded a blue banner in 2001. It's a good place to stop by for a picnic and a swim. Rest here for a few hours before making your return journey. You can also visit the many museums here (*see pp103–5*).

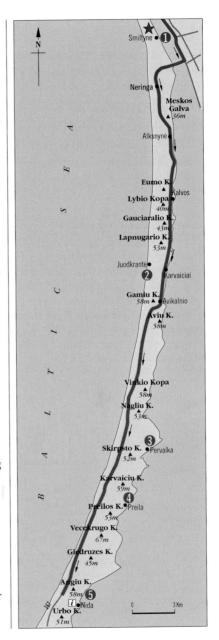

# Northern Lithuania

Northern Lithuania is predominantly agricultural with its share of nature reserves, regional parks, a couple of cities and a host of attractive towns and villages. Although less frequented by tourists, this region has much to offer. Šiaulių, the country's fourth biggest town, is a popular base for visiting the Hill of Crosses. The historic market town of Kėdainiai is attractive and atmospheric and makes a good base for trips to Kaunas and Vilnius.

Only a tiny section of the Hill of Crosses

## Kurtuvėnai Regional Park

This park is only a short drive from Šiaulių, making it a nice and relaxing afternoon trip. A hilly region, it has a mix of lake and forest landscapes. There are a number of outdoor activities on offer for the more energetic. It is a popular area for horse riding. The

Kurtuvėnai Riding Stables organise horse riding as well as cycling trips, educational journeys, riding courses and recreational events. You can also hire bikes and skis here. There is a small hotel if you want to spend the night. Other overnight options are the campsites by the lakes Bijote, Pasvinis

## Northern Lithuania

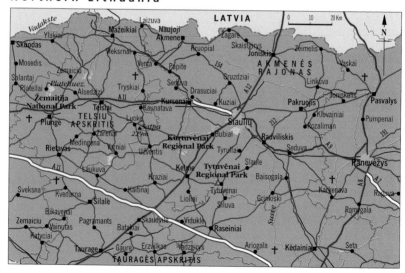

and Geluva and the Dubysa River. It is also a good fishing spot. For more information on the park and activities on offer, email *kurtuva@takas.lt*

### Kryžių Kalnas (Hill of Crosses)

Not to be confused with the Hill of Three Crosses in Vilnius, *(see pp47–8)* this extraordinary place is about 12km from the town of Šiaulių. One of Lithuania's most popular destinations, it has become a symbol of the country's history of suffering and of the people's insurmountable faith as well as their quest for hope and freedom.

Referred to locally as the Hill of Prayers, the Hill of Crosses was originally known as the Jurgaičiai Domantai Mound. It was first mentioned as an archaeological monument in the Register of Lithuanian Cultural Heritage at the end of the 19th century. The mound is thought to have been inhabited since the first millennium AD. A wooden castle stood on it between the 11th and 14th centuries, but this was burnt down in an assault on the community by the Livonian Order in 1348 and never rebuilt.

A number of legends have sprung up to explain why the first cross was put up on the mound. One legend tells of an unhappy father whose beloved daughter was dying. He had been visited in a dream by a woman who told him to make a cross and bring it to the hill by Meškuičių village. The father did as he was bid, carrying to the hill a cross he had made. It took him 13 hours to get there, and when he returned he was greeted by his daughter, who had miraculously recovered. Once word of the miracle spread, people

A sorrowful Jesus weighed down with numerous crosses contemplates the state of mankind

The huge wooden figure of Christ welcomes all who come to pay tribute at the Hill of Crosses

started bringing their own crosses to the hill.

Another version of this legend says that it was a sick man who had simply made a promise to place a cross on the mound if he recovered his health. Another legend says that a manifestation of the Virgin Mary encouraged people to place crosses on the hill.

Whatever the true origin of the legends, the first written record of the site dates from 1850, not long after the 1831 rebellion against the Russians, when many Lithuanians were killed. Their burial places were unknown and it may be that relatives planted the crosses in memory of loved ones who had died. After another rebellion in 1863, the numbers increased further.

The Hill of Crosses began to gain a particular significance during the Soviet Period as a symbol of resistance to the regime. In the mid-1950s, Lithuanians were returning to the country from deportations, and there was a whole new wave of crosses with inscriptions and stories telling of great suffering and losses. Lithuania's history was being chronicled by the crosses. By 1961, there were over 5,000 crosses and the Soviet government decided things had gone far enough. In an attempt to halt the flow of crosses and do away with the site, which symbolised insurrection, the authorities burnt the wooden crosses, destroyed the metal ones, broke up the ones made of stone and threw them into the river. The hill was then flattened with bulldozers and rumours of disease were circulated to justify banning people from the area. The place was put under guard, but still crosses continued to be brought in at

night. Known as 'bulldozer atheism' this pattern continued for nearly 20 years. Despite the destructions, believers continued to visit the hill and even organised pious processions, which were strictly forbidden.

Once the revival of Lithuania had begun in 1988, the future of the hill was assured and the Hill of Crosses became a permanent feature in the Christian world. As a result of Pope John Paul II's holding a Holy Mass at the hill in September 1993, the sacred site became world renowned. Its appeal was further enhanced in 1994, when a magnificent crucifix, a present from Pope John Paul II, was erected on a mound beside the site to commemorate his visit. The church festivals on the Hill have been revived at the foot of this holy gift and the Church Festival of the Holy Cross is held annually on the last weekend of July. The latest addition to this site is a Franciscan monastery built just up the road from the Hill of Crosses in 2000.

Since independence in 1991 the hill has become a monument to the country's defiance and perseverance and a mark to the suffering caused to so many during the years of occupation.

Visiting the hill is an extraordinary experience. In some senses it is an eerie place but in another sense it is a celebration. Although your expectation is of a high hill covered with crosses, that is not in fact what the Hill is. It is a mounded area, not particularly huge and not particularly high. The effect of the experience comes from the density of the crosses. There are tiny haphazard paths threading in and out of the crosses that weave over and around the two

Amber can be bought in many outlets in Šiaulių

*Getting there: 12km from Šiaulių turn off the Rīga road close to the village of Jurgaičiai. Kryžiu Kalnas (The Hill of Crosses) is signposted from the main road and is 2km down this side road. By bus: 5 buses a day from Šiaulių. You have to get off at the Domantai stop and walk the 2km to the site.*

## Šiaulių

Most people only visit Šiaulių as a gateway to the Hill of Crosses, but it is a vibrant city with lots to offer and deserves a visit in its own right. A place with a rich history and a bright future, Šiaulių is the fourth largest city in Lithuania with a population of around 135,000. It was first mentioned in historical documents in the mid-16th century but there had been a settlement here since the 13th century. Šiaulių really came into its own in the 19th century when the Rīga-to-Tilsit road and the Liepāja-to-Warsaw railway line were built. At that time, major industries were established here, including Frenkelis's leather works business. Today, the economy of the city is still dominated by leather processing but other industries also thrive and 90 per

mounds. The occasional solitary cross looks as though it may be trying to make a run for it, but for the most part they are stacked up against each other – different shapes, sizes and materials and hung with smaller versions of themselves. Rosary beads together with messages and photographs that hang from some of the crosses add to the intensity and could be claustrophobic to people with that tendency. The beleaguered wooden Christ near the entrance to the first mound looks as though he is about to fall forward with the weight hanging off him. But every cross has a story and a life attached to it, some happy, most sad. If you visit on a bright sunny day there is a wonder about it; if you visit on a dark, windy day there is a stalwart bleakness to it.

### Churches in Šiaulių
St George's Church, *Kraziu 17*.
St Ignatius' Church, *Vilniaus gatvė 245*.
St. Apostles Peter and Paul's Church of Orthodox Parish, *Rygos 2a*.
St. Apostles Peter and Paul's Cathedral, *Aušros 3*.

### Šiaulių Tourist Information
*Vilniaus gatvė 213. Tel: (370 41) 523 110. www.Šiaulių.lt*

cent of the goods, which include foodstuff and drinks, are exported to Western European countries.

One of the major reconstructions that changed the whole feel of the city was the conversion of Vilniaus gatvė into a pedestrianised zone in the mid-1970s. This was a very innovative move at the time and attracted much interest both within the country and outside. Currently being repaved and modernised, Vilniaus gatvė is one of the most attractive boulevards in the country. Smart shops, restaurants and cafes line the street, somewhat reminiscent of Laisvės Alėja in Kaunas. Overall there is a positive and progressive feel to the city, with its modern shops, cafes and a wide range of hotels.

## Museums

The city boasts a number of unusual museums.

The **Bicycle Museum** has a display of new and old bikes of all shapes and sizes. *Vilniaus gatvė 139. Tel: (370 41) 524 395. Open Tue–Fri, 10am–6pm, Sat 11am–4pm. Admission charge.*

The **Cat Museum** houses a large collection of cat pictures, ornaments, poems and cat-related art work. *Zuvininku 18. Tel: (370 41) 523 883. Open: Tue–Sat 11am–5pm. Admission charge.*

**Frenkel's Palace**, built at the beginning of the 20th century, has one of the most interesting building façades in the city. The interior is in the process of restoration. The palace used to be a

Šiaulių's main shopping street, Vilniaus gatvė

Typical method of conveyance for lake fishermen

Jewish school from 1920–40 and now uses the space for an exhibition on the Jewish history of the region. At present there is a small amount of artwork on display but there are plans to incorporate the entire collection of artwork currently at the Šiaulių Aušros museum with this one which will make it a substantial gallery.

*Vilniaus 74. Tel: (370 41) 524 389. Open: Tue–Sat 10am–5pm. Admission charge.*

**Museum of Photography** For anyone interested in photography the exhibition here has a host of old cameras and examples of the kind of photographs they produced. The collection generally is somewhat limited but the display of photographs of scenes from around the country is interesting particularly if you have been touring through these areas.

*Vilniaus 140. Tel: (370 41) 524 396. Open: Tue–Fri 10am–6pm, Sat 11am–4pm. Admission charge.*

**Radio and TV Museum** This is a pretty quirky museum but contains some extraordinary pieces including a 19th-century musical box with musical bees striking bells and a radio disguised as a toy robot. Also interesting is the demonstration of the Morse code transmitter.

*Vilniaus 174. Tel: (370 41) 524 399. Open: Tue–Fri 10am–6pm, Sat 11am–4pm. Admission charge.*

### Statues

One of the features of Šiaulių is the variety of statues and sculptures dotted around the city. Among these are *Aušra* (*Dawn*), at the intersection of Aušros and Kastonu streets. This statue was erected in the memory of the political and literary group of the 1880s and 90s, called the Dawn Movement. *Grandfather and his Children*, in Priskelimo Square, is a very popular and much loved statue by B Kasperaviciene that is included in the list of Lithuanian cultural monuments. It is a piece crafted on a simple theme but with great charm. Other statues worth seeking out are *Reading Man* by H Orakauskas (*Tilzes 151*), *Sundial* by three local artists, A Cemiauskas, R Jurela and A Vsyniunas, created to celebrate the city's 750th jubilee, and *Three Birds* (*Draugystes 25*) by K Kasperavicius. The last is at the centre of the fountain outside the Šiaulių Hotel.

## Tytuvėnai Regional Park

About 40km south of Šiaulių, this regional park used to be a popular resort for celebrities in the pre-war era. It is now concerned mainly with preserving the cultural and natural environment of the two Catholic centres of Tytuvėnai and Siluva. The park is spread over 10,571ha, with 56 per cent covered in forest and a large proportion of wetlands making it a perfect habitat for many species of birds. It is a very popular destination for dedicated birdwatchers and a number of special hides (watchtowers) have been built in the park to accommodate them. There are also a number of lakes in this park, making it a good spot for fishing. Boats are available to hire; some centres even offer water bicycles.

Tytuvėnai's famous chapel to St Mary is one of five sites in Europe where the apparition of the Virgin Mary is said to have appeared, making it an important pilgrimage site. The first Sunday in September is the day of the pilgrimage and every year thousands of pilgrims make the journey from Tytuvėnai to Siluva.

*Miskininku gatvė 3, LT-5493, Tytuvėnai, Kelmes r., Lithuania. Tel: (370 97) 566 51. email: tytur@pikuolis.omnitel.net*

If you are looking for peace and quiet – here it is

Statue of Alexander, the Great Duke of Lithuania

## Panevėžys

Panevėžys, the capital of Aukštaitija Ethnographic Region, has been the fifth largest city in Lithuania for more than a century. It is situated in the middle of Lithuania; halfway between two Baltic capitals – Vilnius and Rīga. The city lies in a good geographical position which plays a major role in communication with other Lithuanian cities and the city of Kaliningrad. The Via Baltica highway runs through the city and connects it to many Scandinavian and Western European countries.

Today, Panevėžys is a clean, cosy and green city. Incidentally, the inhabitants of Panevėžys are considered to be the oldest pagans in Europe. In 1414 when all Lithuania had already been baptised, priests here were still making sacrifices to old Lithuanian gods in the present place of the Old River Bed. Now the granite monument of Alexander, the Great Duke of Lithuania and the King of Poland, overlooks the panorama of the Old River.

The Old Town of Panevėžys boasts of Laisvės aikštė where modern ideas intertwine with old ones, and Respublikos gatvė famous for its art galleries and snug yellow houses, so unique to Panevėžys.

Some people think of Panevėžys as the city of Juozas Miltinis Drama Theatre, some as the city of the world-famous International Ceramic Symposia; others as the capital of cycling and the Ultra Triathlon where world champions Diana Ziliute and Vidmantas Urbonas were brought up. The city is sometimes called the capital of bicycles and is famous for champions and well-developed bicycle paths, which cover about 100 kilometres.

Local artists, such as actor Donatas Banionis and photographer Algimantas Aleksandravicius, have made Panevėžys famous. The city is also noted for being the home of the Chamber Ensemble Muzika, the Women Chamber Choir Volunge, the Folk Dance Group Grandinele and several upcoming pianists.

Between the World Wars, Panevėžys was famous for its mills. A water mill from 1848, now reinvented as the luxurious Hotel Romantic, has survived.

The favourite hang out in town is the Old River Bed, the site of many a festival. The J Miltinis Drama Theatre is just steps from the Old River Bed. A unique Puppet Wagon Theatre, visiting the remotest Lithuanian towns and villages in summer, is based in the city. The visitor to the city will be curious to see the unique theatre where fantastic puppets live, the café is functioning in a small wagon of narrow gauge railway and the collection of handprints of noble guests is exhibited.

Nearby there is theatre MENAS. In front of it the figure of the great world dreamer and humanist Don Kichot created by the sculptor Henrikas Orakauskas is presented. The sculpture of Don Kichot was made of copper, brass and bronze in accordance to archaic engravings. The butterflies of coloured glass symbolise the fragility of human beings.

There are art galleries and museums besides, and cosy cafes in Laisvės aikštė, the heart of the city.

*Tourist Information Centre, Laisvės a. 11, LT-35200 Panevėžys. Tel: (370 45) 508 081; Fax: (370 45) 508 080, email: info@Panevezys.lt; www.panevezystic.lt*

A celebration in the city of Panevėžys

# The Litvaks

The Lithuanian Jews were known as Litvaks and the majority resided in Vilnius, the capital city of Lithuania. This led to Vilnius becoming known as the 'Jerusalem of Lithuania'. The first mention in the annals of an organised Jewish community in Vilnius is in 1568, when they were ordered to pay a poll tax, and the next significant mention can be traced to February 1633 when the Jews of Vilnius were granted a charter of privileges. This charter outlined their rights and privileges, which permitted them to become involved in all branches of commerce and distilling. It also allowed them to engage in any crafts that were not subject to the guild organisations. The charter did however restrict their places of residence within the city.

The first half of the 17th century saw a steady growth in the Jewish community in Vilnius as immigrants arrived from Prague, Frankfurt and Polish towns. At this time the total population of the city was around 15,000, 3,000 of which were Jewish. These immigrants were often wealthy and educated, and included many famous scholars of Judaism. Over the course of approximately 700 years in Lithuanian history, this Jewish community expanded into a thriving and diverse culture.

## A Centre of Torah Learning

While the Lithuanian Jewish community made up only a small portion of the international Jewish community, it is renowned for its Jewish scholarship. By the beginning of the 17th century Vilnius had already become one of the leading centres for rabbinical studies and was regarded as a centre for Torah learning and culture. Their position in this regard was unique among the Jewish communities worldwide. The Litvaks, in comparison to other European neighbours, constituted a considerably smaller percentage of the domestic population, but they stood out from the other Jewish communities in the calibre of their rational, intellectual approach to learning and spiritual matters as well as in the conduct of their day-to-day affairs.

## The Holocaust

The most terrible era for the Litvaks was during the holocaust in Europe, with the Jewish community sustaining devastating losses at the hands of its occupiers. Over 95 per cent of the Jewish community was wiped out. The Nazi regime is responsible for the annihilation of the Lithuanian Jews, their culture and the destruction of the Litvak legacy. For a comprehensive and stark insight into this genocide, travellers should visit the Museum of Genocide Victims (see pp41–3) in Vilnius. Other smaller local museums in other cities

### FAMOUS JEWISH SCHOLARS BORN IN VILNIUS

Many highly respected Jewish scholars were born and lived in Vilnius in the second half of the 17th century and the beginning of the 18th century. Among these are R Moses, known as Kremer, his son-in-law Joseph, author of Rosh Yosef, Halakhic and Aggadic novellas; R Baruch Kahana, known as Baruch Charif; the grammarian Azriel and his two sons Nisan and Elijah, and Zvi Hirsch Kaidanover.

The second half of the 18th century also boasted many famous scholars that had a profound influence on Judaism. These writers continued to contribute to the religious and spiritual learning as well as the literary reputation of Vilnius and enhanced its reputation as one of the most highly respected centres of learning in Europe at that time. Other famous Lithuanian Jewish scholars included, Joshua Herschel, Ben Joseph and Shabbat Ha-Cohen.

throughout Lithuania also concentrate on the history of these communities. Since Lithuania regained its independence there has been much progress in the revival of the Jewish life and culture and recognition of the suffering that the Litvaks had to endure.

A simple recording of the names of victims on the exterior of the Genocide Victims Museum

# Eastern Lithuania

Eastern Lithuania is dominated by tracts of beautiful landscape punctuated with small towns and national parks that offer historical and specialist museums, a variety of activities and great natural beauty. This is a great area for touring, stopping off in pretty villages, walking or just admiring the scenery. The pace of life is slow and the people friendly and welcoming, eager to share their surroundings. Choose from a range of activities here – walking, riding, swimming, driving, canoeing – the list of things to do is endless.

User-friendly signage in the parks

## The Lay of the Land

The lands of Aukštaitija (the present northeastern and eastern part of Lithuania) were the prime nucleus of the Lithuanian State. Around the 11th century the Duchy of Lithuania was formed here. Due to insightful diplomatic relations it became the most powerful Baltic Duchy in the 12th century when compared to neighbouring Poland and Russia.

Aukštaitija is the biggest ethnographic region of Lithuania. People used to live here in free-planned homesteads or

One of the many recreation centres in Aukštaitija National Park, from where you can hire boats

villages, where the main houses were built along the street and outbuildings were situated in the back yards. The Aukštaitija National Park still accommodates 40 of such exotic 'live' (inhabited) villages. Anykščiai is one of the most attractive small towns within the eponymous region, a beautiful area dominated by lakes. Sirvintos and Molėtai are also worth a visit.

Vivid and bright colours prevail in the traditional textiles and national costumes of this region. People still sing thousand-year-old sutartines of

## Eastern Lithuania

The famous 18th-century wooden Church of St Joseph in Palūšė

Aukštaitija (ancient polyphonic songs). These songs have retained their archaic musical and poetical form. The tunes of these songs witness their ancient origin, and elaborate polyphonic language speaks of the high musical culture of those days. These polyphonic songs represent an exceptional phenomenon not only in Lithuanian but in the world's folklore too. Along with vocal music Aukštaitija people enjoyed original instrumental polyphony performed by pan pipes and horns.

It's hard to tell whether Aukštaitija people started singing or tasting beer first. Aukštaitija, especially Birzai district, is known as the land of brewers. Birzai Castle is home to the Beer Museum and three breweries of the town offer different brands of beer. A big industrial brewery, Utenos Alus, is located in Utena, another town of Aukštaitija. There is a rich culinary heritage in the area, and Aukštaitija is a member of the Culinary Heritage Europe, so if you want to try some traditional specialities of the region just follow the sign 'Kulinarinis paveldas. Aukštaitija' (Culinary Heritage. Aukštaitija).

The Aukštaitija of today is noted for a large variety of dialects, its way of life and ethnocultural heritage, as it has inherited customs and traditions of three big ethnic formations – Sela, Nalsia and Ziemgala. The cheerful temper of the local people is said to stem from the remarkably picturesque scenery, while Aukštaitija is also called the motherland of poets and storytellers.

### Anykščiai

South of the winery town of Anykščiai is the forest of Anykščiai, which is famous for the inspiration it has provided to artists and writers over the centuries. One of the most well-known works of such literature is *The forest of Anykščiai* by Antanas Baranauskas.

While here you must sample the local cuisine as well, which includes delicacies like royal pheasant, deer meat thigh and boar meat rolls. Stuffed pike Aukštaitija-style is a local speciality.

## Aukštaitija National Park

The Aukštaitija National Park is the main attraction in Eastern Lithuania. The park is a mecca for water lovers, cyclists, ramblers and skiers. The majority of the park's territory is pine covered. Some woods are the remnants of ancient forests that once covered a large part of this territory.

The woods, marshes and meadows of the Aukštaitija National Park are full of rare plant species, including protected plants that are listed in the famous *Red Book*. The park contains 100 smaller and larger lakes scattered among the woods and hills.

The park is also known for its rich heritage culture. Within the mounds of Taurapilis, Ginučiai Puziniskiai, Linkmenys and Vajuonis, there are 106 archaeological and architectural features, including the remains of the defence line of the 12th to 15th centuries. The park area also includes over 100 small villages, many of which only contain a few farmsteads. Architecturally, villages in and around the national park fall into three categories: one-street, scattered and detached. One-street villages became the norm in the second half of the 16th century and the structure required farmsteads being laid out next to each other, either on one side of the street or on both. A dwelling house would be constructed perpendicular to the street

with the shed for cattle behind it. The granary for each farmstead would be in front of the dwelling house with the cellar, both forming a separate line and the barn sitting far behind this group. Examples of this structure can be seen in the villages of Ginučiai, Sakaliske and Kretuonys.

Other attractions include **Dringis**, the largest lake in the park (721 ha), **Tauragnas**, the deepest lake in Lithuania (60.5m deep). **Baluošas** lake features seven islands, one of which has a little lake of its own. Of some 30 rivers in the park territory, the **Zeimena** is the most beautiful, although the smaller ones, Kriauna, Lukna, Buka and Sventele are no less attractive to tourists and ethnographers.

This is the place to go if you are into all things ethnographical

The old machinery is still the most reliable

The park territory embraces some 80 settlements and villages, some of which have retained not only their old original layout but also ancient wooden farm buildings and other structures. Of the many towns in this region Ignalina and Palūšė are the most popular with visitors. Palūšė is the tourist centre of the park. It still boasts of an octagonal wooden church dating back to 1757. Palūšė is the starting point for most of the tourist routes, both shorter and longer walks, plus rowing boat trips on the lakes and connecting streams. *Aukštaitija National Park Authority, 4759 Palūšė, ignalinos raj. Tel/Fax: (370 386) 531 35. Admission charge.*

**Ancient Beekeeping Museum**
Set up in 1984 by Bronius Kazlas with the aim of teaching visitors about the history and methods of beekeeping in Lithuania, this Ancient Beekeeping Museum is located on the banks of the Taurgnele

River in Stripeikiai village. Stripeikiai is the oldest village in the Aukštaitija National Park, located in the northwestern part. The museum, on the edge of the Mincia Wood, is one of the most popular attractions in the park. The buildings that house the museum are built in traditional style with thatched

**The Horse Museum**
The only one of its kind in the country, this unusual museum is 6km outside the town of Anykščiai. Founded in 1978, the museum explains the importance of the horse to the economy and culture of Lithuania. Eight different buildings display different equipment, tools and carriages used over the years. There is a play area for children, and there are opportunities to ride a horse or go for a ride in a horse-drawn carriage down the romantic 12km long Stallion Path. A festival of folklore and sports called 'Run, Stallion, Run' is held annually here on the first weekend in June.
*Niuronys Village, Anykščiai District. Tel: (370 381) 517 22.*

roofs. Amongst other things, the museum explains how to protect beehives from bears. Displays include old beekeeping equipment and tools as well as many photographs explaining ancient beekeeping methods. The unusual and intricate woodcarvings around the museum are an attraction in itself. This museum is not too far from Ignalina and if you go via Ginučiai, you can stop and see the famous water mill. On the way back you can take the alternative route back via Palūšė and stop for a swim. *Open: daily 1st May–15th Oct, 10am–7pm; Admission charge (small; reduction for students). For more information www.paluse.lt*

### Ginučiai Water Mill

The one street village of Ginučiai is home to this impressive water mill. Of the six water mills in the Aukštaitija National Park, it is the only one that still has its original equipment. The other five can be found in Pakasas, Gaveikėnai, Pakretuonė, Mincia and Brukninė. The Ginučiai mill is nearly 200 years old and its magical sound reminds you of times past. It was taken out of service in 1968, till which point it was generating electricity for the whole village. If you want to know how to operate such a mill you can learn all about it in the Bread Museum close by. As the name suggests, you can also have a go at baking your own bread here.

If you enjoy fishing, there is an abundance of fish in the lakes of Sravinaitis, Baluošas, Baluosykstis and Almajas, which are all very close to Ginučiai village. This is also a good spot for swimming on a hot summer's day.

You can stay the night for a very reasonable price, in one of the old mill buildings, which have been converted into small self-catering apartments, including a kitchen to prepare your own food. There's also a small restaurant in this attractive rural complex.

The host of the water mill, Algis Gaižutis, is known for telling legends and poems about this area, but beware these may include ghost stories about the mill! During the summer months there is also a food store and snack bar in operation. *Open: daily May–Aug, 10am–5pm; Sep 11am–3pm. Closed: Oct–Apr. Admission charge. Guided tours available. For more information on Ginučiai and other quaint villages in this area, contact the Ignalina or Palūšė information centres, www.paluse.lt; www.ignalina.lt*

### Ignalina

Ignalina is a small town in the Aukštaitija National Park surrounded by numerous lakes and forests with a population of over 7,500 people. It is also the administrative centre of this district. During the second half of the 19th century, the Vilnius–Daugavpils railway line was constructed through this region, leading to increased employment opportunities for the local populace. While the town is within the national park, the entire district is not.

There is an **Ethno Culture Centre** in Ignalina that was opened in 1992. This centre displays folk art collections,

**Ignalina Tourist Information**
*Tel: (370 386) 525 97. www.ignalina.lt*
**Palūšė Tourist Information**
*www.paluse.lt*

ethnographic works, the history of mansions and villages in the region, plus photo archives and biographies of famous people. It also has a craft centre where visitors are encouraged to try their hand at clay pottery.
*Taikos 11. Tel: (370 386) 531 47.*
*Open: Mon–Fri 8am–5pm.*

Ignalina offers many outdoor activities, but you may also simply relax and take in the scenery. In season, Ignalina is an excellent location for winter sports. For more information on activities and accommodation in Ignalina see *www.ignalina.lt*

A forest track near Palūšė

### Palūšė

The village of Palūšė, not far from Ignalina, boasts the oldest wooden church in Lithuania, constructed in the year 1750. The oldest tourist centre in the Ignalina region is also located here. Palūšė is a holiday destination popular with all kinds of people. The information centre is extremely helpful and also provides accommodation in winter and summer. There is also a restaurant within the complex, Aukštaiciu užeiga, which can seat up to 100 people at a time in summer and offers live music on weekends. During the winter a dining room with a capacity of 20 is available.

From Palūšė you can go on day trips by boat, bike or on foot. Other activities on offer include windsurfing, kayaking, canoeing, skiing (in winter), orienteering and tennis, to name just a few. Ignalina is within walking and cycling distance, but even here there are plenty of places close at hand where you can relax by the lakes, take a picnic or walk in the woods.

Other places of interest in the Ignalina district include the **Apiculture museum** in **Stripeikiai**, the **Ginučiai water mill** *(see p125)*, the ethnographic villages of Sakarva and Trainiskis as well as the sturdy oak tree on Baluošas lake (the trunk measures 6 metres in diameter). Other picturesque places in the national park include the Mound of Ginučiai and Siliniskes Crest. You can also relax on the public beach at Gavys lake or enjoy the impressive views from the top of the famous Ledakalnis hill (175m high). Nature comes into its own in this part of the country, and the scenery is just breathtaking. This region

of hills, lakes and forests is the perfect 'getting away from it all' destination. For information on camping, accommodation and activities contact:
*The Ignalina Tourism and Recreation Centre; Tel: (370 386) 525 97 or visit their website www.ignalina.lt*
*Palūšė Tourism Centre; Tel/Fax: (370 386) 528 91, (370 615) 214 01. Email: turizmas.anp@is.lt. Website: www.paluse.lt*

### The Bustling Springs

The town of Alanta, in the region of Molėtai, has a group of natural springs. A project carried out in 2005 by the Society for Making Lithuania Beautiful uncovered 30 springs in this area. They are all registered now. Among the 13 springs that are the main attractions in Molėtai, are the Alanta Parsonage Spring, Ambraziskis Spring, Sarakiskiai Spring and the Diktarai Spring.
*Tel: (370 618) 127 96.*
*Email: irese@omni.lt.*

### Anykščiai

Anykščiai is a winery town in the northeast of the country but can be reached easily as a day trip from Vilnius. It is an extremely attractive market town set around the River Šventoji and has great charm. A little further south you will find the forest of Anykščiai which is famous for inspiring artists and writers over the centuries. One of the most well known works of such literature is by Antanas Baranauskas (1835–1902) called *Anykščiu Silelis* (*Forest of Anykščiai*). There is a museum in the town which honours the country's famous poet – Baranausko ir A Vienuolio-Zukausko memorialinis muziejus (A Baranauskas

and A Vienuolis-Zukauskas memorial museum). This is the first memorial museum of its kind in Lithuania and honours both Baranauskas and the short-story writer Antanas Vienudis Zukauskas (1882–1957), who was a devotee of Baranauskas. The exhibition includes a chair and table that belonged to Baranauskas and some of his manuscripts.
*A Vienuolio gatvė 4. Tel/Fax: (370 381) 580 15, (370 381) 529 12; Open: Mon–Sat May–Aug 9am–6pm Sept–Apr 8am–5pm. www.baranauskas.lt*

The centre of Anykščiai is **Šv Mato Baznycia Anykščiuose (St Matthew Church in Anykščiai)**. Built between 1899 and 1909, it provides the best view of the town. Its main claim to fame, of course, is that it is the highest church in Lithuania, and its two towers, reaching 79 metres, can be seen from miles around. The lofty interior is intricately decorated and the interesting contents include some original side-shrines made of painted wood and a beautiful stained-glass panel by the contemporary artist Anorte Mackelaite.

Before you leave Anykščiai you should make time to go to the winery of which the town is justly proud, the AB 'Anykščiu Vynas' (The Stock Company 'Anykščiai wine'). Visitors are taken on a tour of the winery and factory and to observe the process of wine making. They can then select their own wines for tasting and thereby partake of a selection of the products.
*Darius ir Girėno gatvė 8.*
*Tel: (370 381) 503 13 for opening times and days. There is a charge for the wine tasting but not for entry.*

# Getting Away From It All

Nature in Lithuania is absolutely breathtaking. The country has five main national parks and many regional parks and nature reserves. For travellers looking for respite from the hustle and bustle of crowded tourist sites, these are the places to visit. A number of resorts and retreats offer cures for all types of ailments, physical and emotional, and also that much needed space for oneself to rejuvenate the batteries.

Quirky and often humorous woodcarvings are a feature in many woods and forests

## National Parks

Lithuanian folklore is full of tales of confrontation between human beings and nature. There are stories of people getting lost in dark forests with menacing trails, while others have difficulties with mysterious lakes or battle menacing beasts.

The heroes of these stories, however, never come across as victors over nature. Their victory is always achieved by respecting the land and listening to the animals. As a result of this respect that they show to nature, every creature, big or small, tries to repay them in some manner. Some animals reward the heroes with unusual abilities, while others carry out difficult tasks for them as an expression of their gratitude.

Lithuanians today still respect their land and display a great regard for it – it is part of their national identity. This is expressed in their folk music, dance and art (*see pp20–25*).

The landscapes of Lithuania are not only beautiful, but also extremely diverse. The scenery in the eastern Aukštaitija region, with its chains of lakes, contrasts greatly with the high sand dunes of the Curonian Spit or the dense forests of the Dzūkija region.

The five national parks in Lithuania are: the historical National Park of Trakai, the National Park of Dzūkija, the National Park of the Curonian Spit, the Žemaitija National Park and the National Park of Aukštaitija.

Each park has its own distinctive natural features. Most national parks in Lithuania allow visitors and some even permit camping. However, there are certain reserved areas within the national parks that are not open to visitors unless they are accompanied by the park staff.

The parks offer visitors not only an opportunity to take in some breathtaking sights, including the flora and fauna, but also an opportunity to rest and recuperate. If you are looking for peace and tranquillity, a Lithuanian national park is the place to go.

These visits have a cultural insight to them as well – they will help you understand the Lithuanian culture and people better.

**National Park of Trakai**

The Trakai National Park covers about 8,200 hectares. The Island Castle, located in Trakai, is one of the most famous sites in Lithuania *(see p63)*. This Gothic castle is situated on an island in the middle of Lake Galve.

The town of Trakai was founded in the 14th century and was the second capital of the Grand Duke Kęstutis. Today it remains a beautiful town. The Trakai National Park is probably the most visited of the national parks in Lithuania, and it is easy to see why.

There are 32 lakes within the park, which means that almost one-fifth of the area is water. It is therefore not surprising that many of the activities that the park offers are water-based *(see pp64–5& p158)*. Trakai's close proximity to Vilnius makes it an easy 'getting away' destination for those who may not have the time to travel too far from the main city. Travelling to Trakai from Vilnius is not complicated as there are many buses leaving from the city centre at regular intervals. You can ask at any tourist office for details of timings and routes. It is also easily accessible by car.
*(See Directory, p180, for information on car hire; for more information on Trakai see pp61–5).*

Marshy parts of the national parks and reed beds attract a wonderfully varied birdlife

## Dzūkija National Park

The Dzūkija National Park is close enough to both Vilnius and Kaunas to make it very convenient for a short break. It is only 100km southwest of Vilnius and 100km southeast of Kaunas. This makes it less than an hour and a half's drive from either city. Travelling around the park by car is the most convenient and comfortable method of getting around. The excellent road network provides convenient access to the main areas of Marcinkonys and Merkine.

Organised bus excursions to the park are another option. Detailed information is available at all tourist offices and information centres.

Once there, you can take advantage of the numerous

Trees and more trees

## PLANT KINGDOM, ANIMAL PLANET

The pine trees that dominate the Dzūkija region protect and nurture many a rare and endangered species. In fact, their unique geographical position has determined the region's diversity of species. A combination of sandy plains in the southeast with Dzūkija's moraine highlands, river valleys and a unique climate, has created the habitat for these rare species.

The species list of the region includes 750 types of higher plants, nearly 300 mushrooms, over 200 lichens, 40 mammals, including elk, deer, wild boar, fox and wolf, 48 bird species, 2 kinds of reptiles, 3 of amphibians, 3 of fish, 2 of molluscs, 41 of insects and a type of leech. Of these, 217 species found in this area are on the protected list. These include the eagle owl, the bulbiferous coralwort, the Machaon butterfly and the smooth snake.

walking and biking trails in the park. The park spreads over 55,900ha of southern Lithuania, with 43,700ha of the area under forest cover. Most of it lies in the Varėna district (95 per cent), and small parts in the Alytus district (4 per cent) and Lazdijai district (only 1 per cent).

This national park was founded on 23 April 1991, with the principal objective of protecting, managing and utilising one of the richest natural and cultural territories within Lithuania. It is the largest protected area in Lithuania, with over 30 rivers and streams. Its pine forests are rich in mushrooms and blueberries. But the unique dunes are its core attraction.

The area also contains the remains of some Stone Age settlements. The mounds and hills around Merkine and Liskiava are famous both for their history as well as for their scenic views. The village of Merkine dates back to the 14th century and is situated at the confluence of two rivers, the Nemunas and the Merkys. The castle hill here offers spectacular views of the Nemunas Valley.

The villages of Musteika, Zervynos, Dubininkas and Lynezeris have been listed as national architectural monuments. The traditional layout of these villages, with their typical architecture, has been preserved to this day. Many of the local inhabitants still pursue their traditional crafts of pottery making, woodcarving and weaving.

This rare combination of cultural and natural sights provides the tourist with an array of choices. The lakes are good for swimming, the forests for exploring and mushroom picking and stretches of the rivers Ula and Merkys for canoeing (make sure to purchase a permit for the River Ula, which is available from the park administration). There are also four cycling tracks, six walking and hiking trails and 15 campsites. It is doubtful you can ever be bored here.
*For more information on the Dzūkija Park, email: dzukijanp@is.lt*

**National Park of the Curonian Spit**
The Curonian Spit is a unique piece of land in the west of the country, on the Baltic coast. This national park was created to protect the unique ecosystem of the Curonian Spit, a peninsula that seperates the Kuršių Marios lagoon from the Baltic Sea. The park covers an area of 18,000ha of land.
*For more details on the Curonian Spit, see the section on the Baltic coast, pp100–105 & pp106–107.*

View of the Curonian Spit

Wonderful stretches of pale sandy beaches mark the Lithuanian seaside

On one hand, the Curonian Spit is the land of fishermen, primitive nature and sand dunes. On the other, it is also the place for a tranquil, restful holiday. A lot of new hotels have been built in the last decade, and older ones renovated, attracting more tourists each year, not only from within Lithuania, but from around the world. Tourism has become the main industry in this area. Organising leisure activities in some form or another for tourists is the main livelihood of the 2,700 local people who live in Neringa.

If you get tired of sunbathing on the soft white sands in summer, you can go windsurfing, yachting, biking or boating on the Curonian Lagoon. During the winter, swimming pools are heated, the resorts are quieter and calmer and less packed. Many cafés and bars stay open in the winter, making it a year-round destination. You can also visit the **Ethnographic Fisherman's House**, the **Fisherman's Business Exposition**, the **Thomas Mann Museum**, the **Witches' Hill** with its carved wooden sculptures, the **Amber Gallery**, an ethnographic cemetery and many more interesting places which are open throughout the year. (*See Baltic coast, p88.*)

The Spit is a good 'getaway' destination from Palanga, a popular resort some 30km north, on the coast, which can become a bit of a party town in the summer. There are two regular ferries from Klaipėda city, making it an easy and hassle-free destination, for an

This park is in the northwest of the country, beyond Palanga. It was set up to protect and preserve the natural ecosystem and cultural heritage in the valleys of the rivers Salantas, Erla and Minija. These beautiful old valleys contain springs, ravines and steep escarpments that offer outstanding views. Also interesting to see while you are here are boulders that have remained untouched by civilisation since the last Ice Age (10–12th millennia BC). Most of these can be found around Šaukliai, Kulaliai and Igariai. Tourists come here for outdoor, mainly water, activities. The River Minija is famous for rafting. Both the rivers Minija and Salantas, and the ponds at Mosėdis, offer excellent fishing.

*For more information on this regional park, email:*
*salanturp@kretinga.omnitel.net*

Boats for hire to go fishing or rowing, or to just float in peace and quiet

Sign welcoming you to Žemaitija National Park

afternoon visit or a few days stay if you wish. You can relax on one of the many pristine blue-flag beaches, drive around in a car (*see p176*), or take one of the many organised cruises around the Curonian Lagoon (*see pp100–102*). The two tourist information centres in Neringa give you ample information about local events through literature and booklets. You can make reservations for hotels or private bed-and-breakfast facilities through these centres as well (*see pp170–3*).

## Žemaitija National Park

The Žemaitija National Park is only 33km from the town of Plunge. There are buses and trains connecting Plunge to other towns and cities in Lithuania. The Žemaitija National Park Administration Centre and Visitor Centre are in Plateliai, which can be reached by car or bus. These centres provide information on museums, sites of interest, festivals, accommodation and excursions in the park, and also issue fishing permits.

The landscape of Žemaitija National Park was moulded approximately 12,000 years ago by ice and receding glaciers. These climatic conditions created its distinctive features of rounded hills, deep and shallow lakes, and moraine ridges. There are 26 post-glacial lakes and 32 streams in the park. The largest lake in Žemaitija is Lake Plateliai. The park is a watershed to three river basins, the Minija, the Baetuva and the Venta. The dense forests contain a huge variety of trees, including pine, spruce, birch, alder and oak.

This national park is also famous for its cultural heritage. The 3,000 people that still live in the area have preserved their own particular dialect, customs and characteristics.

There are many museums here, including the **Woodcraft Museum** in Godeliei, the **Literary Museum** in both Bukantė and Žemaičių Kalvarija, and the **Art Gallery** in Babrungėnai.

Activities available in the park include horse riding in Plokstine, which is an easy and relaxing way to enjoy the countryside. You can also hire bikes in Plateliai and take advantage of the three cycling tracks in the park, or hire a boat in Plateliai to either explore the lakes or go fishing.

## Lake Plateliai

This lake is the largest and deepest in the western region (Samogitia) of Lithuania. It covers an area of 1,200ha and at its deepest point is 47m. There are seven islands on the lake, each with its own legends and lore.

There once stood a beautiful castle on

**Diverse and Rare Fauna in Žemaitija National Park**

189 different species of birds have been identified here. 48 are rare species and include the black stork, tern and corncrake. There are 49 species of mammals, 13 of which are protected, including the lynx, otter and white hare. There are 11 species of bats here and 26 species of fish, including rare members of the salmon family. Some have existed in Lake Plateliai since the post-glacial era. There are over 600 species of beetles and 640 species of butterflies too.

Sunlight streams through the trees, creating a picturesque canvas of light and shade

Lakeside accommodation in the national parks

---

### FESTIVALS AND EVENTS IN THE ŽEMAITIJA NATIONAL PARK

| | |
|---|---|
| **Shrove Tuesday Carnival** | February or March |
| **Europarc's Day** | End of May |
| **The Midsummer Folk Festival** | 23 June |
| **Church Festival in Žemaičių Kalvarija** | First two weeks of July |
| **Swimming competition in Lake Plateliai** | Last Sunday in July |
| **Rock nights** | Beginning of August |
| **Plateliai Regatta** | End of August |
| **Tourism Day** | End of September |

the largest of the seven islands, but now only its ruins remain. Three of the islands and one of the peninsulas have been declared national natural monuments. The hills around the lake provide excellent views of the water and the islands in it. The forest and surrounding marshes are home to unique flora and fauna.

The lake landscape itself offers crystal-clear water, clean campsites and beautiful scenery.

The region has many bays, peninsulas and walking routes that can be explored by foot, bike, boat or car. In Plateliai town, there are some shops, cafés, hotels, a petrol station and a post office, making it a good place to stop for the night, to relax, refuel and rejuvenate.

The town also houses the management office of Žemaitija National Park, the Local Authority office and a tourist information centre, so it is a good place to pick up information on the rest of the park.

### National Park of Aukštaitija

Aukštaitija National Park, established in 1974, was the first of Lithuania's national parks. This protection has helped the park sustain many species of plants and animals, including a single specimen of the rare ghost orchid.

Situated in the northeastern region of the country, its proximity to Vilnius (only 70km away), makes it a popular destination. You can either hire a car (*see Directory, p180*) or take a bus.

National Park of Aukštaitija

Spread over 40,570ha, this natural paradise is made up of rolling hills, 102 lakes, both large and small, and 34 rivers and streams. Most of the lakes lie next to each other, forming a sort of unlinked chain.

A hundred-odd settlements dot the park, most of them housing a few farming families. Most of these settlements are said to be over 2,000 years old.

Any description of this area of the country must contain the word 'sparkling'. This amount of water provides many opportunities for water-based activities, such as canoeing and fishing (it is necessary to purchase a fishing licence, available from any of the tourist centres or the nearest forestry office).

The best way to travel within the park is by boat, as the numerous forest paths inevitably lead to the water's edge. This way, you can explore the more remote and untouched areas.

There are countless options for beautiful lakeside walks and to revel in the stunning scenery of the rolling hills and beautiful forests that surround the lakes. A walk up to the top of Ladakalnis Hill is well worth the effort for a bird's-eye view of the entire park.

The area is great for birdwatching. Along the edge of the water, you can often spot birds like black-throated divers, black storks, curlews and snipes feeding.

An abundance of apples in September

Long, straight roads cut through the forests throughout the country

This park also offers many adventure activities in the winter, including cross-country skiing, ice-fishing, sledging and horse- and sleigh-riding.
*For more information on Aukštaitija National Park, contact the Aukštaitija National Park Authority: 4759 Palūšė, Ignalinos raj. Tel/fax: (370 386) 531 35; email: anp@is.lt.*

### Ignalina and Palūšė
Ignalina is a small town in Aukštaitija National Park; Palūšė is a village close by and also the administrative centre for the park (*see Eastern Lithuania, pp125–7*). Both towns offer accommodation and good local cuisine, and either would make a good base out of which to explore the park.

# Shopping

Shopping in Lithuania has plenty to offer. There are many souvenir shops which offer traditional products, amber and woodcarvings. The main cities provide the option of shopping in European and American clothing chains. There are also many shops for fine cosmetics and perfumes in the cities. The fashion ranges from traditional to funky. Whether you are looking for local products, souvenirs, handbags, fur or leather, you will find it in Lithuania, especially in the larger cities.

A sign often seen throughout the country

Regular shopping hours are weekdays 10am–7pm, Saturdays 10am–3pm; some shops are open on Sundays as well. Food stores are usually open between 8am and 10pm; some supermarkets are open until midnight. There are also a few shops which are open 24 hours.

Street vendors under the arches in Vilnius

### Amber
Baltic amber, as much as 50 million years old, is a tourist attraction in itself in Lithuania. It has been considered the most valuable Lithuanian export for centuries, traded as far as ancient Rome. An amber souvenir is said to bring good luck. It is especially valuable if there is an insect trapped inside the resinous gem. The Old Town in Vilnius is the best place to go, but remember to get a certificate of origin for your purchase.

### Souvenirs
There is a wide range of interesting souvenirs you can bring back from Lithuania. The country has a strong tradition of handicrafts, be it in woodcarving, linen or woven sashes. Beautiful handmade sashes represent a very old part of Lithuanian tradition, as they used to be worn instead of belts. The array of colours used in these sashes reflects the Lithuanian appreciation for bright colours. They are no longer used solely as belts, but are available in many lengths and widths, so you can make

them into unusual interior decoration features. Handmade mittens and socks are also nice gifts to take home. The knitted 'flax' tablecloths are also extremely popular.

**Fashion**

Vilnius and Kaunas have the most cosmopolitan choice in fashion, with a number of upmarket European brands represented here. However, it is always worth scouting around in smaller cities and towns, as you never know where you may come across something unusual – something that you would not find at home – which is always part of the joy of shopping when you are on holiday abroad.

**VILNIUS**

Shopping in Vilnius city centre and the Old Town is best done on foot. Head for Gedimino, Pilies, Didžioji, Aušros Vartų, Vokiečių and Vilniaus streets. You can find all the international brands in the Old Town and on Gedimino Prospektas shopping area, as well as antiques, crafts, art and books. If you are looking for local craft and souvenirs in particular, visit the street markets on Pilies and Didžioji gatvės.

There are a variety of souvenir and craft shops in this area. Along Pilies gatvė there are many outdoor stalls which supply all types of souvenirs, including amber, woodcarvings, handmade toys and jewellery. The main

Handmade toys on display at a stall

concentration of clothes and shoe shops can be found on Gedimino Prospektas.

## Art, Handicraft and Antique Shops

**Antikvaras** (antiques)
*Pilies g. 32-4.*
**Antikvaras** (antiques)
*Pilies g. 21.*
**Keramikos Meno Centras** (ceramics)
*Kauno g. 36/7.*
**Kleišmantas IR KO** (jewellery)
*A Vienuolio g. 14.*
**Linas** (linen)
*Stikliu g. 3; Didžioji g. 11.*
**Lithuanian Craftsmen Union Gallery**
*Stikliu g. 16.*
**Suvenyrai** (souvenirs)
*Šv Jono g. 12.*
**Verpste** (handicrafts)
*Zydu g. 2.*
**Vilnius Antique Centre** (antiques)
*Dominikonų g. 16.*

## Books

**Akademinė Knyga**
*Universiteto g. 4.*
**French Bookshop**
*Didžioji g. 21.*

Some highly unusual amber pieces are for sale

**Humanitas**
*Vokiečių g. 2.*
**Littera**
*Šv Jono g. 12.*
**Oxford Centre**
*Trakų g. 5.*

## Shopping Centres

If you are looking for international and local fashion, essential services, restaurants and cafés, as well as plenty of leisure activities all in one place, try one of the modern shopping centres. The centres listed here all have on-site parking.

**Europa**
Over 80 stylish shops. Plenty of cafés, restaurants, salons and other services.
*Konstitucijos pr. 7A.*
**Akropolis**
Over 120 stores, a supermarket and an entertainment centre.
*Ozo g. 25.*
**VCUP**
Over 100 stores, restaurant, bar, bistro and a broad range of other services.
*Konstitucijos pr. 16.*

## Amber

In and around the Old Town is considered the best place in Vilnius to buy the coveted Baltic amber. However, do beware of fakes. Buy only from stores which provide a certificate of origin with the sale.

**Amber**
*Aušros Vartų g. 9.*
**Amber Museum Gallery**
*Šv Mykolo g. 8.*
**Gintaras**
*Didžioji g. 5.*

**Mažasis Gintaro Muziejus**
*Didžioji g. 6.*

## KAUNAS
The main shopping spine of the city is to be found along Vilniaus gatvė in the Old Town, running into Laisvės alėja in the New Town. You will find a huge range of shops here, plus stall traders selling anything from souvenirs to sunglasses and second-hand books.

### Antiques
**Viktorija**
*Gruodžio g. 4.*

### Gifts and Souvenirs
**Dovanu Salonas**
*Laisvės al. 110.*
**Kauno Langas**
*Vilniaus g. 22.*
**Suvenyrai**
*Vilniaus g. 32.*

### Clothing & Accessories
**Aprangos Galerija**
*Laisvės al. 55.*
**Baltman**
*Laisvės al. 49.*
**Jackpot & Cottonfield**
*Laisvės al. 80.*

> **Tax Refunds**
> In Lithuania it is possible for all foreigners, who are not European Union residents, to get a tax refund if you spend more than 200lt (approximately 58euro) in one store. The rate of exchange is currently at 18 per cent. However, this is only available in shops that display the sign TAX FREE SHOPPING. In these shops, ask for a tax money return form and a tax invoice. You must also remember to get a stamp on the invoice from your point of departure.

Brightly coloured wooden fish make a good gift to take home

**In Wear-Matinique**
*Laisvės al. 69.*

### Food and Drink
**Arbata, Prieskoniai, Kava**
*Vilniaus g. 29.*
**IKI**
*Jonavos g. 3.*

### Books
**Humanitas**
*Vilniaus g. 11.*
**Knygų Alėja**
*Laisvės al. 29.*
**Septynios Vienatves**
*Daukšos g. 31.*

## KLAIPĖDA
Leave your clothes, shoes and accessory shopping for Vilnius and Kaunus, and in Klaipėda concentrate on the whimsical. There are several quirky shops, perfect for buying unique gifts to take home.

**Bičių Korys**
Delicious local honey.
*Sukilėlių g. 18.*

**Cronus**
Leather goods.
*Vytauto g. 3/28.*

**Jūros Dovanos**
Gifts from the sea and a choice of amber.
*Kepėjų g. 8a.*

**Kriaukes ir Koralai**
Coral and shells.
*Tomo g. 10.*

**Laimės Tiltas**
Clocks and watches at reasonable prices.
*Tiltų g. 4.*

**Mažoji Indija**
Exotic pieces from Africa and the East.
*Tomo g. 16-1.*

**Žemaitija**
Hand-painted clothes, wooden carvings
and other unusual objects.
*Aukštoji g. 5.*

**ŠIAULIŲ**
The wide pedestrianised main street,
Vilniaus gatvė, is lined with shops and
cafés. This is where you will find the
majority of good shops. It is a good
place to look for unusual souvenirs
and gifts.

**Dorado**
Plenty of choice here for gifts – some
sophisticated, some not.
*Vilniaus g. 215.*

**Lėja**
Good selection of accessory-type items.
*Vytauto g. 110.*

**Savex Galerija**
An extraordinary and eclectic array of
unlikely goods.
*Vilniaus g. 251.*

**Tourism Information Centre**
Interesting assortment of souvenirs and
craft items.
*Vilniaus g. 213.*

A beautiful collector's item – an amber rickshaw with a passenger

# Amber

Legend and science tell different stories about the origins of amber. Lithuanian legend holds that amber originates from the tears of the sea goddess Jūratė. She fell in love with a mortal fisherman, Kastytis, and invited him to come and live under the sea in her beautiful castle of amber.

When Perkunas, the god of thunder, found out about this love affair, he was very unhappy. In a fit of anger, he destroyed her castle with a storm. Pieces of amber found today are supposed to be the remains of her castle and her tears.

Science tells another, not so romantic story of amber's origin. Approximately 40–50 million years ago, the earth got warmer, which led to an increase in the amount of resin secreted in the pine forests of Fennoscandia. This large land mass was later consumed by the Baltic Sea. The resin was then swept down the rivers to the sea, with its sticky properties sometimes catching an insect or even a lizard along the way. Deltaic deposits of this fossilised resin are what we know as amber and can be found in Lithuania, Poland, Sweden and the Kaliningrad region in Russia.

There are many amber museums in the main cities that illustrate the story of the evolution of amber. The largest collection of rare pieces of amber in the world can be found in the Tiškevičius Palace, on the outskirts of Palanga. This fine mansion was bought by Count Felix Tiškevičius in the 1850s and is a great setting for this fascinating museum. The exhibition is very well presented and gives a comprehensive and clear history of the origins of the substance. You can see 25,000 examples of the different types of amber, many with plants, animals and insects trapped inside. There is a magnificent array of jewellery and other items too.

Amber is popularly known as Lithuanian gold and can still be found on the shores of the Baltic Sea, particularly after a storm. Although the majority of pieces are clear, the ones that contain the remains of an insect or a pine needle are the most valuable. Amber is the classic Lithuanian souvenir to bring home to any member of your family. There is a vast range of crafted pieces to choose from, including necklaces, bracelets, rings and other jewellery, unusual ornaments and lamps. Amber comes in a whole range of colours, the most common being a dark honey colour, but it is also found in blue, deep red, orange, black, white and yellow. It is important to get a certificate of origin and authenticity for your purchase, as there are many fakes around.

Amber museums are located throughout Lithuania. Enquire at the local tourist offices for recommendations in their region.

# Entertainment

Lithuania has a rich cultural heritage in both classical and contemporary art, music and drama. Vilnius and Kaunas both have regular programmes of concerts and operas running throughout the year, including many jazz festivals (*see pp26–7*). Folk music and dance are also an important part of the entertainment scene, but performances tend to be more ad hoc. In the cities across Lithuania, there is no shortage of mainstream nightlife, which includes clubs, discos, cafés and bar music.

Jazz group entertaining guests at a restaurant

The main concentration of casinos and strip clubs are in Vilnius. Local publications contain current information on events and venues to cater to all tastes and predilections. Cinemas countrywide feature recent film releases, generally in the original language with Lithuanian subtitles (*see local press/publications for details*).

## Vilnius
### CLUBS AND DISCOS
**Brodvejus Pub**
European pub/bar with a disco and a great live music club. Entrance charge is balanced by free drink vouchers.
*Mesiniu g. 4.*
*Tel: (370 5) 210 72 08.*
*Open: daily noon–3am,*
*Sat noon–5am.*
**Cozy**
Attractive, intimate little bar/club in the heart of the Old Town.
*Dominikonų g. 85.*
*Tel: (370 5) 261 11 37.*
**Pabo Latino**
This popular Latin-themed club where you can tango or salsa attracts a more sophisticated clientele than some of the other nightclubs.
*Trakų g. 3/2.*
*Tel: (370 5) 262 10 45.*
*Open: Thur–Sat*
*11am–5am.*
**Prospekto Pub**
Offering a variety of music every night of the week, it also has a comfortable lounge area on the third floor.
*Gedimino g. 2.*
*Tel: (370 5) 262 20 19.*
*Open: 11am–5am.*

### CASINOS
**Casino Planet**
Quite a relaxed atmosphere with friendly dealers – not over the top.
*Basanaviciaus g. 4.*
*Tel: (370 5) 269 11 40.*
*Open: Fri 4pm–4am, Sat*
*4pm–6am.*
**Grand Casino World**
Completely the other end of the spectrum from Casino Planet, this place is everything you would have expected a casino to be. Spread over three floors, with restaurants, bars and gaming tables.
*Vienuolio g. 4.*
*Tel: (370 700) 555 99.*
*Open: daily 24 hrs.*
**Olympic Casino**
There are a number of branches of the Olympic Casino around the city. This is one of the largest and is the nearest to a

Vegas-type of experience you will get.
*Konstitucijos pr. 20 (Reval Hotel Lietuva).*
*Tel: (370 5) 231 49 30.*
*Open: daily 24 hrs.*

## OPERA, MUSIC & BALLET

**Opera and Ballet Theatre**
Keep an eye on the local press for performances taking place here. It is worth visiting anyway for the exceptional venue alone.
*Vienuolio g. 1.*
*Tel: (370 5) 262 07 27;*
*www.opera.lt*

## THEATRES

**Lele Puppet Theatre**
A great place to take children. Very

experienced late-1950s puppet company.
*Arklių g. 5. Tel: (370 5) 262 86 78. Open: Tue–Sun 10am–4pm.*
**National Drama Theatre**
Look in the local press or see the billboard outside for details of performances. Notice the Three Muses guarding the entrance.
*Gedimino g. 4.*
*Tel: (370 5) 262 97 71.*

## GALLERIES

**Alternatyvaus Meno Centras** (Alternative Arts Centre)
*Užupio g. 2.*
*Tel: (370 5) 262 00 83.*
**Art Academy Gallery**
*Pilies g. 44/2.*
*Tel: (370 5) 261 20 94.*

**Artists' Palace**
*Didžioji g. 31.*
*Tel: (370 5) 261 75 72.*
**Contemporary Art Centre**
*Vokiečių g. 2.*
*Tel: (370 5) 262 98 91.*
**Gallery of Russian Culture Centre**
*Boksto g. 4/2.*
*Tel: (370 5) 215 38 75.*
**Lietuvos Aidas' Gallery**
*Universiteto g. 2.*
*Tel: (370 5) 212 47 27.*
**Prospektas Gallery**
*Gedimino pr. 43.*
*Tel: (370 5) 261 16 65.*
**Užupio Galerija**
*Užupio g. 3.*
*Tel: (370 5) 231 23 18.*
**Znad Wilii** (Polish Gallery)
*Isganytojo g. 2/4.*
*Tel: (370 2) 223 020.*

The Three Muses outside the National Drama Theatre

## CINEMAS

If you have access to the internet while you are here, log on to *www.cinema.lt* to see what's on offer around the capital.

**Forum Cinema Coca Cola Plaza**
*Savanorių pr. 7.*
*Tel: (370 5) 264 47 64;*
*www.forumcinemas.lt*
**Lietuva**
*Pylimo g. 17.*
*Tel: (370 5) 262 34 22;*
*www.ktlietuva*
**Skalvijos kino centras**
*A Goštauto g. 2/15.*
*Tel: (370 5) 261 05 05.*

## Kaunas

## CASINOS

**Olympic Casino**
*Donelaicio g. 27.*
*Tel: (370 37) 409 962.*

## CINEMAS

**Planetą**
*Vytauto pr. 6.*
*Tel: (370 37) 338 330.*
**Romuva**
*Laisvės al. 54.*
*Tel: (370 37) 324 212.*

## DANCE

**Kaunas Dance Theatre Aura**
*M Daukšos g. 30a.*
*Tel: (370 37) 202 062;*
*www.aura.lt*

## GALLERIES

**Gallery**
*Vilniaus g. 10. Tel: (370 37) 209 774; Open: Mon–Fri 10am–6pm, Sat 10am–4pm.*
**Gallery of Lithuanian Artists Association**
*Rotušės al. 27.*
*Tel: (370 37) 337 166.*
**Gallery Meno Parkas**
*Rotušės al. 27.*
*Tel: (370 37) 337 167; Open: Mon–Fri 11am–6pm, Sat 11am–4pm.*
**Gallery of the Guild of Textilists and Artists**
*Naugardo g. 9–1.*
*Tel: (370 37) 201 366. Open: Tue–Sat 10am–6pm.*

Europa has world-class clubs and discos

Jazz festival in Vilnius

**Kauno Langas**
*Valančiaus 5. Tel: (370 27)*
*205 538; Open: Mon–Fri*
*10am–6pm, Sat*
*10am–4pm.*
**Fujifilm Gallery**
*Rotušės al. 1.*
*Tel: (370 37) 321 789.*
*Open: daily 11am–5pm.*
*Closed: Mon.*

**OPERA, MUSIC &**
**BALLET**
**Kaunas Centre of**
**Religious Music**
*Vsj Maironio g. 14-16.*
*Tel: (370 37) 228 213.*
**Kaunas Musical Theatre**
*Laisvės al. 71.*
*Tel: (370 37) 228 784.*
**Kaunas Philharmonic**
*L Sapiegos g. 5.*
*Tel: (370 37) 327 427.*

**THEATRES**
**Kaunas Academic Drama**
**Theatre**
*Laisvės al. 71.*
*Tel: (370 37) 224 064;*
*www.dramosteatras.lt*
**Kaunas Musical Theatre**
*Laisvės al. 91.*
*Tel: (370 37) 228 784.*

**BOWLING**
**Oazė**
*Baltų pr. 16.*
*Tel: (370 37) 755 012.*
*Open: Mon–Wed*
*11am–midnight,*
*Thur–Sat 11am–2am.*
**Straikas**
*Draugystės g. 6a.*
*Tel: (370 37) 409 000.*
*Open: Mon–Fri*
*noon–3am, Sat & Sun*
*11am–3am.*

**CLUBS & DISCOS**
**Amerika Pirtyje**
*Vytauto pr. 71. Tel: (370*
*37) 201 489. Open:*
*Sun–Wed 11am–2am,*
*Thur 11am–3am, Fri*
*11am–4am, Sat noon–4am.*
**Europa**
*Gruodžio g. 19.*
*Tel: (370 37) 302 711.*
*Open: Mon*
*11am–midnight,*
*Tue–Thur 11am–3am,*
*Fri 11am–4am, Sat*
*noon–4am, Sun*
*noon–midnight.*
**Los Patrankos**
*Savanorių pr. 124.*
*Tel: (370 37) 338 228.*
*Open: Tue–Thur*
*8pm–4am, Fri 10pm–6am,*
*Sat 8pm–6am, Sun*
*2pm–5am.*

Enactment of a play at the O Korsunavas theatre

**Metelica**
A branch of the well-known and sophisticated Russian nightclub.
*Laisvės al. 46a.*
*Tel: (370 655) 099 88.*
*Open: Wed, Fri–Sat 9pm–6am, Thur 9pm–3am.*
*Closed: Sun–Tue.*
**Siena**
*Laisvės al. 93.*
*Tel: (370 37) 424 424.*
*Open: Wed 9pm–2am, Thur–Sat 9pm–4am.*
**Zepelinus**
Nightclub with a billiards hall in the back.
*Kovo 11-osios g. 22.*
*Tel: (370 600) 227 22.*
*Open: Mon 11am–11pm, Tue–Thur 11am–3am, Fri 11am–5am, Sat noon–5am, Sun noon–11pm.*

**CASINOS**
**Olympic Casino**
*Donelaicio g. 27 (Takioji Neris hotel). Tel: (370 37) 409 962. Open: 24 hrs.*

**Klaipėda**
**THEATRES**
**Drama Theatre**
*Teatro 2. Tel: (370 46) 314 453; www.kidteatras.lt*
**Musical Theatre**
*Danes g. 19.*
*Tel: (370 46) 397 404; www.muzikinis-teatras.lt*

**CONCERT HALLS**
**Philharmonic**
*Danes g. 19.*
*Tel: (370 46) 410 576.*

**GALLERIES**
**Exhibition Hall**
*Aukštoji g. 3. Tel: (370 46) 314 443. Open daily:*

*winter 11am–7pm, summer 10am–6pm.*
**Fotogalerija**
*Tomo 7. Tel: (370 46) 410 122. Open: Tue–Sat noon–5pm.*
**Klaipėda Picture Gallery**
*Liepu g. 33. Tel: (370 46) 410 412. Open: Tue–Sat noon–6pm, Sun noon–5pm.*
**Parko Galerija**
*Turgaus g. 9.*
*Tel: (370 46) 310 501; www.parkgallery.com.*
*Open: Mon–Fri 11am–5.30pm, Sat 11am–3pm.*

**CINEMAS**
**Jūratė ir Kastytis**
*Talkos pr. 105.*
*Tel: (370 46) 342 857.*
**Žemaitija**
*Manto g. 31.*
*Tel: (370 46) 314 090.*

Pavement cafés are popular in the summer

# Children

While there are not many attractions specifically designed for children in Lithuania, they will not be short of things to do. The Baltic coast offers all the usual beach-related activities and water sports. The national parks are crammed with things for children to do from boating and walking to visiting folk museums and outdoor playgrounds. There are plenty of child-friendly facilities throughout the country, including designated play areas at beaches, parks, cities and service stations.

Plenty of well-signposted walking trails

You can also find crèches and play areas in most shopping malls. It is worth noting that journeys around the country by public transport can be lengthy, so if you are taking a long-distance train or bus, remember to take along plenty of books, games, snacks and drinks.

### Hotels, Restaurants and Cafés

Children are welcome in most hotels, restaurants and cafés. Hotels offer good value for family rooms and some of the large, modern hotels have child-

Fishing in peace and solitude in a wonderful setting

minding facilities. Restaurants often offer children's menus or will provide half portions on request. Some provide play areas for children. There are also some specifically child-oriented places to eat.

### Beaches

Palanga is the premier beach resort on Lithuania's Baltic coast offering a wide sandy beach and good swimming. There are water sports, pedaloes and plenty of other amusements for children available in this fun resort. The Curonian Spit, around 80km south of Palanga, has a long dune-fringed beach on its western shore; the eastern side faces the Curonian Lagoon, with water sports, including canoeing and sailing, on offer.

### Bicycling

The flatness of the land makes cycling a perfect pastime for the whole family. For information on hiring bikes, cycle maps, tours, repairs and anything else you need to know about bikes, log on to this great site: *www.bicycle.lt*

## Ice-Skating and Sledging

In winter, there are many opportunities around the country for ice-skating and sledging. Ask at local information centres for details of what is available in the area.

## Water sports

A huge variety of water sports are available for children countrywide. These include seaside water sports such as swimming, surfing and sailing and, in the national parks, there are many other water-based sports such as rowing, canoeing and swimming. Ask in the local information offices for details of what is on offer.

The following listings cover the main attractions for children in Vilnius, Kaunas and Klaipėda.

## VILNIUS
### Child-Friendly Cafés
**Kvepsė**
*Konstitucijos pr. 25.*
*Tel: (370 5) 275 43 93.*
**Kvikio klubas** (at Europa shopping centre)
*Konstitucijos pr. 7A.*
*Tel: (370 5) 248 71 04.*
**Laukiniai vakarai**
*Antakalnio g. 66.*
*Tel: (370 5) 234 39 80.*
**Nykatuku pasaulis**
*Laisvės pr. 88.*
*Tel: (370 5) 240 70 70.*
**Skrajos kavinė**
*Naugarduko g. 55A.*
*Tel: (370 5) 233 55 04.*

Traditional woodcarving

## Cinema

The four main cinema complexes in Vilnius show the latest European films in their original languages with Lithuanian subtitles.
**Forum Cinemas Akropolis**
*Ozo g. 25. Tel: (370 5) 248 48 48.*
**Forum Cinemas Coca Cola Plaza**
*Savanorių pr. 7. Tel: (370 5) 264 47 64.*
**Lietuva**
*Pylimo g. 17. Tel: (370 5) 262 34 22.*
**Skalvijos kino centras**
*A Goštauto g. 2/15.*
*Tel: (370 5) 261 05 05.*

## Indoor Playgrounds
**Euroopa** (at Akropolis shopping centre)
*Ozo g. 25. Tel: (370 5) 238 78 48.*
**Europa Shopping Centre**
*Konstitucijos pr. 7A.*
*Tel: (370 5) 248 71 04.*
**Isdykelio sala**
*Naugarduko g. 97.*
*Tel: (370 5) 213 58 41.*
**Mauglis**
*Žirmūnų g. 1e.*
*Tel: (370 5) 273 53 49.*
**Nykstuku pasaulis**
*Laisvės pr. 88.*
*Tel: (370  5) 240 70 70.*

## Other Places of Interest
**Lithuanian Railway Museum**
A quaint little museum covering the history of the railway in Lithuania. Children will particularly like the train set on display.
*Mindaugo g. 15. Tel: (370 5) 269 37 41. Open: Tue–Sat 9am–5pm.*

For the modest to change in privacy

## Sport and Leisure
**Ice Palace**
*Azuolyno g. 5. Tel: (370 5) 242 44 44.*
*Open: 8am–10pm.*

## Theatres and Puppet Shows
**Elfų teatras**
*Konstitucijos pr. 23b.*
*Tel: (370 5) 272  60 52.*
**Keistuolių teatras**
*Laisvės pr. 60. Tel: (370 5) 242 45 85.*
**Lėlės teatras**
*Arklių g. 5. Tel: (370 5) 262 86 78.*
**Raganiukės teatras**
*Vilniaus g. 22. Tel: (370 5) 276 92 60.*

## KAUNAS
### Cinemas
**Galerijos kinas**
*Nepriklaumybes al. 12.*
*Tel: (370 37) 222 853.*
**Planetą**
*Vytauto pr. 6.*
*Tel: (370 37) 338 330.*

**Romuva**
*Laisvės al. 54. Tel: (370 37) 324 212.*
**Senasis trestas**
*A Mickevičiaus g. 8A.*
*Tel: (370 37) 796 982.*

### Zoo
Not a magnificent zoo but the only one in the country. It contains over 250 different species.
*Radvilenu pl 21. Tel: (370 37) 332 540.*
*Open: May–Aug, daily 9am–7pm.*
*Sept–Apr, 9am–5pm.*

### Sport and Leisure
**Kaunas Children and Student Leisure Palace**
*Parodos g. 26. Tel: (370 37) 423 205.*
**Kaunas Young TC Centre**
*Gedimino g. 13. Tel: (370 37) 422 750.*
**Kaunas Swimming School Silainiai**
*Balyu pr. 8. Tel: (370 37) 377 842.*
**Kaunas Swimming School Vilija**
*Demokratu g. 34a. Tel: (370 37) 362 091.*

**Ledo Arena Ice Skating**
*Aušros g. 42C. Tel: (370 37) 330 675.*
*Open: variable.*
**Orange Tennis Centre**
*Pasiles g. 39a.*
*Tel: (370 37) 764 626; www.otc.lt*
**Yachting and Diving Centre**
*Pramones pr. 15. Tel: (370 37) 764 390.*

**Theatres and Museums**
**Children and Youth Theatre Vilkolakis**
*Kovo 11-osios g. 108. Tel: (370 37) 313 712.*
**Devil Museum**
*Putvinskio g. 64. Tel: (370 37) 221 587.*
*Open: Tue–Sun 11am–5pm.*
**Kaunas Puppet Theatre**
Next door to the puppet theatre is a
'small' restaurant designed for 'small'
people. There are a variety of large
colourful toys for kids to play with.
*Laisvės al. 87a. Tel: (370 37) 313 712.*
*Open: Sat noon–5pm, Sun 11am–1pm.*
**Museum of Children's Literature**
*K Donelaicio g. 13. Tel: (370
37) 206 488. Open:
9am–5pm.*
**Pantomime and Plastic
Art Theatre**
*E Ozeskienes g. 12. Tel:
(370 37) 423 668.*

**Klaipėda**
**CINEMAS**
**Jūratė ir Kastytis**
*Taikos g. 105. Tel: (370 46)
342 857.*
**Žemaitija**
*Manto g. 31. Tel: (370 46)
314 090.*

**Other Places of Interest**
**The Aquarium**
This large aquarium is housed in a
former fort. The aquatic species on
display range from very small fish to
dolphins and penguins. In order to get
there, you have to take the Smiltyne
ferry, which adds excitement to the
outing. When you arrive, you walk along
the riverbank to the right.
*Smiltyne pl 3. Tel: (370 46) 490 751;
ljm@juru.muziejus.lt. Open: Jun–Aug,
Tue–Sun 10.30am–6.30pm; May & Sept,
Wed–Sun 10.30am–4.30pm; Oct–Apr,
Sat–Sun 10.30am–4.30pm.*
*Guided tours in Lithuanian, English,
German and Russian.*
**Blacksmith's Museum**
*Saltkalviu g. 2. Tel: (370 46) 410 526.*
*Open: Tue–Sat 10am–5.30pm.*
**Clock and Watch Museum**
*Liepu g. 12. Tel: (370 46) 410 413.*

**Sport and Leisure**
**Gintaras Swimming Pool**
*Daukanto 29. Tel: (370
46) 410 968. Open:
6am–10pm.*
**Klaipėda Sports
Centre**
*Gulbiu 8. Tel: (370 46) 215 275.*
*Open: Wed, Fri–Sun
8am–11pm.*
**Outdoor Tennis Court**
*Donelaicio g. 6a. Tel: (370 46)
412 102. Open: 7am–10pm.*
**Stalo Tenisas**
**SportoKlubas** (Table
Tennis) *Daukanto g. 24.
Tel: (370 46) 410 905.*
*Open: Mon–Fri 3–9pm.*
*Pre-booking of facilities advised.*

Funny fish – a park sign

# Sport and Leisure

Lithuania is blessed with large areas of outstanding natural beauty and this is reflected in the local population's enthusiastic participation in outdoor sports and activities. As a consequence of this, there are many miles of designated trails for cycling and hiking. Lithuanian tourism is still relatively undeveloped, so the visitor might find that detailed information on areas outside the main cities is hard to come by. However, with a little perseverance you can enjoy some stunning landscapes in relative tranquillity.

Permits are compulsory for fishing

Lithuania's many and varied national parks and countryside provide the perfect setting for horseriding, fishing and other activities. Lithuania is also a nation with strong traditions in team sports with basketball in particular verging on a national religion. In addition to these land-based activities, Lithuania boasts many facilities for rowing, canoeing and sailing on its numerous pristine lakes. For the less adventurous, hiring motorised boats is a popular and affordable option.

Of the three Baltic States, Lithuania is best known as a sporting nation, mainly based on the strength and popularity of its national basketball league. Other significant professional sports are football, cycling and athletics, but the main focus remains on basketball which consistently draws the largest crowds.

### Basketball

Lithuania's association with basketball began in 1920, when national aviation hero Steponas Darius (*see p84*) returned to the country after a period living in the USA. Darius was responsible for introducing many sports to Lithuania but it was basketball that really caught the local imagination. In 1922 he established the national basketball league and the game has gone from strength to strength ever since. Žalgiris Kaunas is the dominant force in Lithuanian basketball and the team have won the European championship several times.

The Lithuanian Basketball Federation organises the national league and provides details of teams and fixtures: *www.krepsiniofederacija.lt*

Tickets for basketball matches in Lithuania are available online or by telephone from the company Tiketa: *Tel: (370 37) 208 683; www.tiketa.lt*

The main basketball stadium in Vilnius is the Siemens Arena, home to Lietuvos Rytas basketball team, more information is available here: *www.siemens-arena.com*

## Cycling

In many ways the Lithuanian countryside is perfectly suited to exploration by bicycle – its undemanding terrain, low levels of traffic, extensive network of surfaced roads and ever-changing landscape makes cycling a joy. Various companies offer organised cycling tours and this is an increasingly popular option for many travellers.

However, with a little research independent bicycle trips are relatively easy to organise and offer peace and tranquillity in picturesque surroundings. Many cyclists pass through Lithuania as part of a wider tour of the Baltic States.

The most well-known route is the Baltic Coast Cycle Route (EuroVelo route No 10 from Bûtingë to Nida), covering the whole length of Lithuania's Baltic coastline. This route takes you through the beautiful Pajûrio Regional Rark and from 2006 it will also run along the coast of the Curonian Lagoon to the Nemunas Regional Park. There are also marked cycle routes in Žemaitija National Park and Kurtuvënai, Nemunas Loops and Panemunës Regional Parks (*www.travel.lt*).

Cycle hire, repair and cycling supplies are readily available in many towns and the non-profit organisation Du Ratai (Two Wheels) will even let you hire a bicycle in Lithuania and return it in Estonia or Latvia. The Lithuanian Cyclists' Community (LCC) represents the interests of cyclists in Lithuania. Du Ratai can be contacted via email at: *info@bicycle.lt* or alternatively via their partners in Lithuania:

### Vilnius
### BaltiCCycle
*PO Box 61, LT 01002 Vilnius.*
*Tel:(370 699) 560 09*
*email: BaltiCCycle@bicycle.lt,*
*Frankas@bicycle.lt, info@dviratis.lt,*
*www.bicycle.lt*

### Klaipėda
*Tourism and Culture Information Centre*
*Turgaus g. 7 (in the Old Town)*
*Tel: (370 46) 412 186*

### Kaunas
*Aciu Rusys (Bicycle Celler) /*
*Gintarius ir co.*
*Misko g. 30*
*Tel: (370 37) 208 76*
*www.dviratis.lietuvoje.info*

### Lithuanian Cyclists Community
*PO Box 190, LT 91001 Klaipëda.*
*Tel: (370 615) 917 73;*
*email: info@bicycle.lt; www.bicycle.lt*

## Fishing

Lithuania offers excellent opportunities for a wide range of fishing and this is a great way to enjoy the country's unspoiled lakes and rivers. Coarse fishing (for carp, tench, bream and the like) is popular, and Lithuania is also home to some of Europe's best pike fishing. Fly-fishing for trout and grayling is also good, and numerous companies offer fully inclusive fly-fishing holidays. The fishing season runs from April to November, although it should be noted that there are short restrictions on fishing for certain species within this period. Hardy anglers can try ice-fishing in the winter months on Lithuania's numerous frozen lakes. Vodka is traditionally consumed in liberal quantities to keep the cold at bay.

Active Holidays offer organised ice-fishing trips that include all the necessary safety equipment and permits; this may be the best option for the novice.

To fish in public waters in Lithuania, you must first obtain a fishing permit. Permits can be purchased from fishing shops and fishing clubs and these are also great places to get advice on local conditions. Note that salmon and trout can only be fished in specific regions and a special licence is required. These licences are issued by the Department of Water Resources (*Juozapaviciaus g. 9, Vilnius; Tel: (370 5) 272 37 86*).

### Active Holidays
*Rodunios kelias 8, Vilnius LT-02187.*
*Tel: (370 687) 218 47;*
*www.activeholidays.lt*

### Football
Lithuania does not have a strong tradition in football, but this is rapidly changing as the sport grows in popularity. International matches are played at Žalgiris Stadium in Vilnius (*just north of the river in central Vilnius, Rinktines g. 3*). For more information contact the Lithuanian Football Association (*Seimyniskiu g. 15; Tel: (370 5) 263 87 41*).

### Hiking
Lithuania is ideal for hiking as the majority of its terrain consists of rolling hills and there are numerous regions of outstanding scenic beauty. A quarter of the land area is forested and there are five national parks and many other conservation areas and regional parks. There are miles of hiking trails in nearly

Cycling is popular in Lithuania

all of these parks and the wider countryside. One of the highlights is Aukštaitija National Park, a vast area of pine forests and lakes, interspersed with 80 historic Lithuanians villages. Many routes follow the rivers that wind through the park. The Curonian Spit National Park is another favourite – there are walks along the unique landscape of the spit including areas of large sand dunes and several pine forests. The spit is also an excellent location for mushrooming – a popular activity in Lithuania. Trakai National Park provides the perfect location for a day trip from Vilnius – it is located just 25km from the city and surrounds the historic town of Trakai, a major attraction in its own right.

### Health Clubs and Gyms in Vilnius
**Antilope Sporto Klubas**
In Ýverynas, across from the Viktoria Hotel. Has an aerobics studio and a well-equipped gym. This club is aimed at women in particular.
*Saltoniskiû g. 29. Tel: (370 5) 279 00 29.*
**Body Gym**
Holds aerobic sessions with qualified local instructors.
*Olimpieciu g. 3. Tel: (370 5) 272 77 44; www.bodygym.lt*
**Forum Sports Club**
Everything you would expect from a large health club: gym, pool, saunas, aerobics, massage, solarium, etc.
*Konstitucijos g. 26. Tel: (370 5) 263 66 66; www.forumpalace.lt*
**Grožio Terapijos ir Kosmetologijos Centras**
A modern and professional beauty studio that offers a wide range of treatments such as dermatology and a host of other skin

and body treatments you may or may not have heard of. They also hold a range of aerobics classes and have a pool complex with saunas and Jacuzzis. The centre features a large workout room and hotel.
*À. Sugiharos g. 3. Tel: (370 5) 270 57 10; www.sugihara.lt*
**Le Méridien Villon Fitness Centre**
One of the best fitness centres in Vilnius. Rooms all have pleasant views of a tranquil lake and birch forest. As you might expect, there is a pool, Jacuzzi, aerobics and weight rooms. Open to non-residents.
*20km from Vilnius on the A2 (the Vilnius-Rīga highway), inside the Le Méridien Villon Hotel. Tel: (370 5) 273 97 77; www.hotelvillon.lt*
**Olympic Gym**
A contemporary and popular gym with aerobics, Jacuzzi, pool and sauna.
*Ozo g. 41. Tel: (370 5) 240 09 60; www.olympicgym.lt*

---

**SPORT CENTRES**
**Ice Palace** (Ledo Rumai)
This ice rink has a capacity of up to 400 skaters and seating for 3,000 spectators.
*Azuolyno g. Vilnius 5. Tel: (370 5) 242 44 44.*
**Lietuvos Telekomas Sports Club**
*Savanorių g. 28 Vilnius. Tel: (370 5) 260 37 57; www.telecomsportsclub.lt*
**Prosperas Horseriding**
*Gineitiske Village. Tel: (370 5) 231 90 07; www.horse.lt*
**Vilniaus Aeroklubas** (skydiving)
Offers parachute jumps from Russian aircraft at various altitudes. Beginners must take a compulsory 3-hour training course.
*Kyviskes g. Vilnius Tel: (370 5) 232 57 18.*
**Winter Sports Centre, Ignalina**
Has cross-country skiing trails in winter and a new ski jump. The trails are great for biking, hiking and running in the summer.
*30127 Sporto g. 3, Ignalina, Tel. (370 29) 541 93.*

# Food and Drink

Lithuania offers a wide range of delicious natural foods. Traditional dishes are prepared according to season and with what nature provides. In every restaurant you will find traditional dishes, and in most, a range of European and international cuisine. Many places offer a wide range of game dishes, prepared according to age-old recipes.

Fried bread sticks with lashings of garlic

## What to Eat

### Appetisers
In most pubs and restaurants the appetiser menus vary depending upon what you are drinking. For example, there are different cheese plates on offer to accompany beer and to go with wine. Bar food that accompanies beer includes smoked or boiled pig's ears, fried bread with an abundance of raw crushed garlic and often smoked chicken stomachs. Other entrees may include boiled tongue, vegetables in crispy beer batter or smoked fish. Most of these dishes are eaten with fried crackling bacon and sour cream.

Traditional veal dish with vegetables

Don't worry, for those of you who would rather stick to what you know, there is a wide range of international restaurants to choose from, including Chinese, Japanese, Hungarian, French, Italian, Spanish and Scandinavian. Most traditional restaurants also offer a range of European and American-style dishes. Seafood dishes, which on the whole are extremely good, are available in all restaurants.

Fixed-price meals, *kompleksiniai* in Lithuanian, are available in many restaurants and cafés and are normally much cheaper than items on the à la carte menu.

### Traditional Dishes
Each region of Lithuania prepares different local dishes, depending on the local produce available in that area. However, in almost every restaurant in the country you will find traditional dishes.

Cold beetroot soup *saltibarsciai*, is

### Beer
Freshly brewed, unpasteurised beer is a local speciality in Lithuania. It is customary in most bars to have some food appetisers with your pint.

probably the best-known traditional dish in Lithuania. This refreshing and filling dish usually contains raw eggs and is accompanied by a dish of potatoes. It is also served hot, more in line with the Russian version of beetroot soup – *borscht*.

Pork is the most popular meat and almost every part of the animal is consumed. The ears and trotters as very popular appetisers, and pork fillets in breadcrumbs called *karbonadas* feature on most menus.

The proximity of the Baltic Sea and the Curonian Lagoon means that fish is plentiful in Lithuania and is served in most restaurants. On the Curonian Spit you will find roadside stalls selling a variety of smoked fish (*see p103*).

Another popular traditional dish is *lietiniai*, sometimes also referred to as *blynelia*. These are pancakes and are made with various sweet and savoury fillings. A dish that you will find in all restaurants is *naminės salotos*. It is a traditional Lithuanian salad made of boiled potatoes, carrots, peas and other ingredients and is cheap but extremely filling.

## Vegetarian Food

The humble potato is the primary source of food in Lithuania and provides the average Lithuanian with their staple diet. There are a number of national dishes that use the potato as their main constituent. For example *bulviniai blynai* which is made from raw potato, passed through a very fine grater, combined with egg and then blanched in very hot oil. Another popular potato-based vegetarian dish is

Cheese and olive appetiser

kugelis – this comes in the shape of a small slab of mashed potato cooked in the oven. *Cepelinai*, found in most restaurants is a local dish of zeppelin-shaped packages filled with the *bulviniai* mixture and can be stuffed with mushrooms or cheese to suit the vegetarian palate and dropped into boiling water (they are also available with meat for the carnivore).

Pasta is also popular and easily found as well as pancakes filled with a variety of vegetarian-friendly fillings.

Most of these vegetarian dishes do not come with additional vegetables and are extremely filling in their own right.

Almost all of the restaurants in the main towns and cities would include a vegetarian option or two in addition to the above mentioned dishes which would be universally available in restaurants serving traditional and general European food.

## Desserts and Cakes

Lithuanian desserts are not particularly creative. Mixed fruit, ice cream and

Restaurant/bar sign in Vilnius

**ALITA**

Alita was set up as a company in 1963 and is based in Alytus. It produces a range of sparkling wines, fruit and grape wines, brandy and concentrated apple drinks. Alita's sparkling wine is their most famous product, which they first produced in 1980. The majority of their products are made from local resources such as apples and berries. The grapes used for the sparkling wine are imported from Moldova and other countries. In order to reduce the production time from three years to three months Alita have managed to develop a biochemically altered version of the French *méthode champenoise*. Such technological advances have led to a steady rise in the quantity, quality and variety of wines produced by Alita.

Alita produce 10 different products which include:

- **Auksinis (Golden):** a sparkling wine of yellowish colour with a gold shade. It has a mild taste with a hint of vanilla and chocolate flavour and takes six months to mature.
- **Karalius Mindaugas (King Mindaugas):** a splendid festive drink, truly called the King of Wines. It is a sparkling grape wine, produced from the Cabernet grape. After storing and souring, the sparkling wine matures and gains a stronger flavour and a pleasant taste.
- **Brandy Alita:** the newest of Alita's products.

Alita has won awards for its quality and significant achievements in trade with the EU countries.

pastries are the most popular. With the advent of the café in the main cities though, the pastry and cake business is thriving and you will never be short of a place to satisfy a craving for sugar.

## What to Drink

### Coffee (Kava)

Excellent coffee is found all across Lithuania. The coffee is usually of very good quality and served with care. Italian coffee is probably the most frequently served, but there is a wide range available.

### Spirits

There are a number of Lithuanian spirits and a good way to get a taste of them is to ask for the Merry Rolling Pin. This is a paddle designed for entertainment and a chance to taste a variety of Lithuanian spirits at one sitting. The Merry Rolling Pin is served in most bars and restaurants and allows you to try six different Lithuanian spirits at one go.

### Wine

The reason you have not heard of Lithuanian wine before is because it is not generally very good. However, they do have their own sparkling wine

**Wine Prices**

Wine can be expensive in restaurants. Even if the rest of the menu appears reasonable, check out the wine list. Also be aware that wine measurements vary according to the restaurant, and often are served in 33ml measure, which can be disappointing if you are expecting a full glass!

which is of good quality and a little more famous. Alita is the local sparkling wine that is produced in the town of Alytus (*see p162*). Most red and white wines are imported. Chilean wine is a favourite with Lithuanians. You can also buy French, Spanish and Australian wines in most restaurants but they are expensive.

**Beer (Alus)**

There are many local beers of high quality available all around Lithuania. In the cities you will find brewery-style restaurants, that pride themselves on brewing their own beers. These include light beers, natural bread cider, and half-dark honey beers of unique taste. These unpasteurised beers are a must-try for any visitor to Lithuania. There are a

The Merry Rolling Pin

number of breweries around the country and unsurprisingly, beers tend to be a speciality of their particular region.

Traditional Lithuanian food includes beer, bread and smoked sausages

A minimalist city café

## Where to Eat

The price range below indicates the price of a meal per person, without wine.

| ★★★★★ | over 80lt |
|---|---|
| ★★★★ | 65–80lt |
| ★★★ | 50–65lt |
| ★★ | 40–50lt |
| ★ | under 40lt |

### Smoking

There are only a very few non-smoking restaurants in Vilnius and the other cities but some places provide separate dining areas for smokers and non-smokers. If it is important to you, it is best to telephone the restaurant in advance.

### Vilnius

Restaurants in Vilnius have come a long way in recent years. For a capital full of people who love bland spice-free food, Vilnius has an incredible range of ethnic restaurants: Chinese, Greek, Indian, Japanese, Thai, Lebanese. Be warned that many Lithuanian restaurants tend to serve extra-large portions, fit for a small army. In addition to standard restaurants, Vilnius also abounds in cheap cafeterias or *valgy klas*. These sometimes suspect meat-and-potato places are frequented by students, pensioners and others in search of inexpensive filling meals.

### Achtamar ★★

One of the best places for Georgian and other Caucasian dishes in the country. The meat is excellently cooked but beware, the portions are huge.
*Konarskio g. 1.*
*Tel: (370 5) 233 13 44.*

**Auksinis Feniksas** ★★★
You need to reserve a table in this excellent, if expensive Chinese restaurant, not only because of its popularity and the standard of its food, but because the restaurant is tiny.
*Gedimino pr. 64.*
*Tel: (370 5) 249 69 09.*

**Čili Kaimas** ★★
This is part of the extremely successful Lithuanian restaurant chain which concentrates on traditional dishes in a fun atmosphere for good prices. The staff are not

Stylish presentation of delicious food

always as efficient as you might like and the decor a bit too traditional, but the food is good.
*Restaurants at:*

*Vokiečių g. 8.*
*Tel: (370 5) 231 25 36.*
*Pirmunų 2 (inside IKI Minskas).*
*Tel: (370 5) 273 54 73.*

Restaurant and microbrewery in Klaipėda

A restaurant in historic surroundings

Designer chicken

*Ukmergės g. 282*
*(inside Maxima).*
*Tel: (370 5) 238 83 84.*
**Cosy** ★★★
This small café/restaurant
is situated in the heart of
Vilnius Old Town. As the
name implies, it provides
a cosy atmosphere. It
provides an excellent
breakfast menu as well
as satisfying lunches,
and a dinner menu that
offers mainly European
dishes
*Dominikonų g. 10.*
*Tel: (370 5) 261 11 37.*
**Les Amis** ★★
Charming and very good

French bistro.
*Savičiaus 9-1.*
*Tel: (370 5) 212 37 38.*
**Le Paysage ★★★★**
Even if you are not
staying at the hotel, this
fine restaurant is worth a
trip. French cuisine, a
beautiful view of a lake
and a birch forest, and
excellent service.
*Off the Vilnius–Rīga*
*highway (A2) in the*
*Le Méridien Villon Hotel,*
*a 20-minute drive from*
*the city.*
*Tel: (370 5) 273 96 00.*

**La Provence ★★★**
A lovely setting and really
delicious Mediterranean
cuisine. A visit to this
restaurant is a must.
*Vokiečių g. 22.*
*Tel: (370 5) 261 65 73.*
**Literatų Svetainė ★★★**
An extremely
sophisticated Swedish
restaurant. Delicious food
exceptionally well-
presented.
*Gedimino pr. 1.*
*Tel: (370 5) 261 18 89.*
**Sorena ★★**
Delicious Azerbaijani

cuisine in a laid-back
atmosphere. Once again,
the meat is cooked to
perfection and the variety
of dishes will bring you
back again and again.
*Islandijos 4.*
*Tel: (370 5) 262 75 60.*
**Stikliai Aludë ★★**
Good traditional food,
often accompanied by live
Lithuanian folk music in
the beer hall. The wine
cellar downstairs is quaint
and quieter.
*Gaono 7.*
*Tel: (370 5) 262 45 01.*

A beautifully presented desert

**Klaipėda**

**Black Cat 2 ★★**

A spacious bar close to the river, popular with expats and offering a decent international menu. Hitler is reputed to have dined here in 1939.
*Zveju 21/1.*
*Tel: (370 46) 411 167.*

**Čili Kaimas ★★**

Traditional Lithuanian dishes are served inside a renovated Soviet cinema. Being Klaipėda, the theme is aquatic, from the full-on decor to a separate seafood menu.
*Manto 11.*
*Tel: (370 46) 310 953.*

**Čili Pica ★**

A huge choice of good pizza and pasta dishes that don't disappoint. Home delivery and takeaway available.
*Taikos pr. 28.*
*Tel: (370 46) 222 222.*

**Navalis Café ★**

Fabulous coffee and snacks. Great people-watching windows too.
*Manto 23.*
*Tel: (370 46) 404 200.*

**Kaunas**

**Medziotoju Užeiga ★★★**

There are two parts to this excellent restaurant: the very classy dining room area and a more relaxed bistro area. Food served in both is of the same high standard. Very expensive wine list.
*Rotušės al. 10.*
*Tel: (370 37) 320 956.*

**Metų Laikai ★★★**

Relaxed atmosphere with rustic decoration. Interesting food includes blue shark.
*Mickevičiaus g. 40b.*
*Tel: (370 37) 223 253.*

**Trakai**

**Apvalaus Stalo Klubas ★/★★**

Separate areas in this

Lithuanian brown bread and white cheese with honey

Beer bar and restaurant in Vilnius

restaurant, depending on your dining style. A great place to see sunset views of the castle.
*Karaimu 53a.*
*Tel: (370 528) 555 95.*

**Csárda ★★**
This Hungarian-style restaurant is a little out of the way, but worth it for its good range of meat and fish dishes, wine and Hungarian vodka.
*Aukstadvario 28a.*
*Tel: (370 528) 539 08.*

**Kybynlar ★★**
It doesn't look great outside but don't be put off. Inside, it is stylish and offers a wide

range of dishes, many traditional.
*Karaimu 29.*
*Tel: (370 528) 55 179.*

**Nida**
**Baras Po Vysniom ★**
Tiny wooden cabin offering a small menu of simple but well-cooked food. Atmosphere unfussy and cosy.
*Nagliu 10.*
*Tel: (370 469) 529 06.*

**Seklycia ★★/★★★**
Probably the most formal restaurant in Nida, serving excellent food, particularly the soups and fish. The rooftop terrace

offers great views of the dunes.
*Lotmiskio g. 1*
*Tel: (370 469) 500 01.*

**Palanga**
**Molinis Ąsotis ★**
Large wooden cabin with seating inside and out. Good, reasonably priced local dishes.
*Basanaviciaus g. 8.*
*Tel: (370 460) 402 08.*

**Monika ★**
Also on the main street, this neat and relaxed bistro serves pizzas and traditional food.
*Basanaviciaus g. 12.*
*Tel: (370 460) 525 60.*

# Hotels and Accommodation

Lithuania has accommodation to suit all tastes and pockets. In the main cities there are a variety of upmarket de luxe hotel chains, mid-range hotels, rented apartments, bed and breakfast accommodation, budget accommodation and hostels. In the more rural parts of the country there is a range of cheaper and less fancy rented apartments, hotels and bed-and-breakfast-style accommodation in local farmsteads. Booking in advance is recommended during peak season.

Bed & breakfast is an economical option

Bed and Breakfast establishments in Lithuania are more like B&Bs in the USA than their English equivalent. In Lithuania this is most likely to be an apartment rather than the small cosy hotel or guesthouse type you would expect in the UK. It is wise to check out the rooms first before checking in.

## Where to Stay

The following list of suggested hotels will help you select an appropriate place to suit your budget. Price guide is the B&B price per person sharing.

★    Budget: €50
★★    Moderate/ Standard: €50-75
★★★    Expensive: €75-100
★★★★    Luxury: €100+

### VILNIUS

**Artis ★★**
In an excellent location between the Old Town and Gedimino, this is a very comfortable, well-run hotel with a popular bar and restaurant.
*Liejyklos 11/23.*
*Tel: (370 5) 266 03 66.*
*www.centrumhotels.com*

**Atrium ★★**
An extremely civilised hotel right in the heart of the Old Town. There is a wide choice of rooms and some spacious apartments.
*Pilies g. 10. Tel: (370 5) 210 77 77. www.atrium.lt.*

**Comfort Vilnius ★**
This relatively new hotel is simple, clean, cheap and centrally located. Continental breakfast only.
*Gėlių 5. Tel: (370 5) 264 88 33. www.comfort.lt.*

**Domus Maria Guesthouse ★**
Right in the heart of the Old Town close to the Gates of Dawn, this simple but pristine B&B is in a former Carmelite Monastery.
*Aušros Vartų g. 12. Tel: (370 5) 264 48 80. http://domusmaria. vilnesis.lt.*

**Shakespeare ★★★**
This hotel feels more like an English club rather than a hotel and is extremely comfortable. Rooms are all individually decorated and named after a Shakespearian character.

*Bernardinų g. 8/8.*
*Tel: (370 5) 266 58 85;*
*www.shakespeare.lt.*

## Trakai
### Trakai Sport Centre Hotel ★★
The location couldn't be better, on the lakeside, so try to get a room with a view of the lake or the castle. Activities on offer include ice-fishing, parachuting and ballooning.
*Karaimo 73.*
*Tel: (370 528) 555 01.*
*www.sc.trakai.com.*
### Akmeninė Užeiga ★★
This hotel is behind Trakai and near the

Akmena Lake, it is a little hard to find so it is probably best to call for directions first. The setting is fabulous, on the Akmena Lake, some say the finest of all Trakai's lakes, and it is worth the effort of looking for it.
*Brazuloles Village.*
*Tel: (370 614) 866 54.*
*www.akmenineuzeiga.lt.*

## Alytus
### Senas Namas ★
Hotel Senas Namas was originally established in 1997 but was completely renovated and expanded in 2004. The hotel is very quiet despite the fact that

it is situated in the very centre of Alytus town.
*Uzuolankos g. 24.*
*Tel: (370 315) 534 89.*

## Druskininkai
### Druskininkai Hotel ★★
Excellent hotel with a small spa right in the centre of the resort only 50metres from Druskonis Lake.
*V Kudirkos g. 41.*
*Tel: (370 313) 525 66.*
*www.hotel-druskininkai.lt.*
### Sanatorium Egle ★★
Sanatorium Egle offers newly renovated rooms and full service including three daily meals and five treatment procedures.

A traditional Lithuanian home converted into a guesthouse

The Druskininkai Hotel has a small spa

Perfect for relaxation or an overnight stay.
*Egles g. 1.*
*Tel: (370 313) 602 22.*

**Regina ★★**
In a quiet but central part of the resort, this hotel is a great base for the area. Rooms are neat and spacious with all the modern facilities you need.
*T Kosciuskos g. 3.*
*Tel: (370 313) 590 60.*
*www.regina.lt*

**Hotel Spa Vilnius ★★**
The most modern health, treatment and rehabilitation centre in Druskininkai, with a great choice of spa services, a four star hotel, beauty institute and many other facilities for relaxation and rejuvenation.
*K Dineikos g. 1, Druskininkai.*
*Tel: (370 313) 538 11;*
*www.spa-vilnius.com.*

### Kaunas

**Kaunas Hotel ★★★**
This is probably the most luxurious hotel in the city and the only one on Laisvės Avenue, the city's main street.
*Laisvės al. 79.*
*Tel: (370 37) 750 850.*
*www.kaunashotel.lt.*

**Marija Karpenko Apartments ★**
Incredibly good value, spacious and comfortable. Right in the centre of town and with secure parking, these apartments make an excellent base for visiting the city and touring.
*J Gruodžio g. 17.*
*Tel: (370 37) 323 123.*
*www.crumina.lt*

### Klaipėda

**Europa Palace ★★**
This is luxury accommodation with a personal touch. It is in an excellent location on the most attractive square in the Old Town.
*Zveju 21/1.*
*Tel: (370 46) 404 444.*
*www.hoteleuropa.lt*

**Hotel Klapieda ★★**
It has had a complete overhaul since the Soviet days and is an excellent and extremely convenient

place to stay. Don't be put off by its appearance.
*Naujo Sodo g. 1.*
*Tel: (370 46) 404 372.*
*www.klaipedahotel.lt*

**Litinterp Guesthouse ★**
This cosy guesthouse is located on the historical Puodziu gatvė in Klaipėda Old Town. The house is newly renovated and has 11 spacious, carpeted and comfortably furnished rooms of various sizes.
*Puodžių g. 17.*
*Tel: (370 46) 411 814.*
*www.litinterp.lt.*

**Palanga**

**Alanga ★**
Just off one of the main boulevards and only a few minutes walk to the sea, this is a quiet and relaxed place to stay. Spacious modern rooms with good facilities. It is possible to do your own catering if you prefer to do so.
*S Neries g. 14.*
*Tel: (370 460) 492 15.*
*www.alanga.lt.*

**Mama Rosa Villa ★**
Mama Rosa is a modern three-floor villa-type building with a classic English interior. Located in the centre of Palanga but on a quiet residential street it is an extremely comfortable and convenient base for the area.
*Jūratės g. 28A.*
*Tel: (370 460) 485 81.*
*www.mamarosa.lt.*

**Austėja ★**
Clean, simply furnished, good-sized rooms are not the only reason that makes this hotel a good place to stay. It is on a quiet street but close to the sea and all the attractions. Excellent value.
*Smilciu g. 31.*
*Tel: (370 460) 543 50.*

**Šiaulių**

**Saulys ★★★★**
New, smart, modern hotel with 39 rooms, located in the city centre of Šiaulių. The hotel has a nice restaurant, conference room and a sauna with a swimming pool.
*Vasario 16-osios g. 40,*
*Šiaulių. Tel: (370 41) 520 812. www.saulys.lt.*

The ultra-modern Hotel Spa Vilnius

# Practical Guide

### Arriving

Arriving in Lithuania has become relatively trouble-free, especially by air. If you are travelling by car you can expect to be delayed up to a few hours at the Russian (Kaliningrad) and Belarus borders. The delays that used to be experienced at the Latvian and Polish borders have reduced considerably in the last few years.

### Visa and Entry Formalities

European Union citizens do not require a visa for entry into Lithuania. In fact, they can live and work in Lithuania without a visa for unlimited periods. Visitors from the following countries

can enter for 90 days stay within a 12-month period without a visa: United States of America, Canada, Australia, New Zealand, Switzerland and all the Nordic countries. Visas cannot be obtained at the border, so it is important to check if you require one before you travel by contacting the Lithuanian diplomatic authority in your country. For a comprehensive online list of the countries requiring visas, look up *www.urm.lt*

Alternatively, you can contact the Consular Department of the Ministry of Foreign Affairs for more information *Tel: (370 5) 262 01 47; Fax: (370 5) 212 27 05.*

Rail junction in Northern Lithuania

Klaipėda, on the Baltic Sea, is Lithuania's main port

## By Air

**Vilnius:** Vilnius Airport, where most international flights arrive, is Lithuania's main and busiest airport. There are now direct flights from 24 European cities, including Dublin, Frankfurt, London and Paris. Although not direct, one of the popular routes is through the Nordic and Scandinavian cities. There are no direct flights to Lithuania from Australia, New Zealand or North and South America. The other main airports are situated in Kaunas and Klaipėda.

There are plenty of taxis available at the airport, which is only 5km from the city centre (15–20 minutes, sometimes a hair-raising journey). You are best off taking one which identifies its company and number on the car, and establishes a price at the outset. A cheaper alternative is to take one of the buses that stop in front of the arrivals hall. Bus No 1 stops outside the train station, Bus No 2 goes to Lukiskiu aikštė on Gedimino prospektas, the city's main street. (*see www.sas.lt, www.airbaltic.com, www.aerlingus.ie*)

**Kaunas:** The airport is situated 12km north of the city. It is a small airport and not very busy so you can be out of there very quickly. There are plenty of taxis waiting but make sure you settle on a fare beforehand. Minibuses also do the short trip to the centre and charge considerably less. (*For details of routes and timetables of Air Lithuania flights, see www.airlithuania.lt*)

**Palanga/Klaipėda:** Klaipėda airport is 25km north of the city and about 25km south of Palanga, and so relatively convenient for both. Scheduled buses from the airport to the city coincide with incoming flights and give you about half an hour to board after the flight lands. Taxis are not always available.

It is also possible to fly to Rīga in Latvia and drive across the border, although check with the car hire company if you intend to do this as there may be cost implications.

## By Bus

There are regular bus routes from various European cities direct to Vilnius, and it is a reasonably comfortable, cheap way to travel although it will obviously add considerably to your travel time. (*Details of routes and timetables can be found on www.eurolines.lt*)

## By Car

There are a number of ferry connections from northern Europe, the UK and France. To plan the best route take the Lithuanian port of Klaipėda as your final destination and then work back from there, depending on time available and your preferred route. The motorway network through Belgium and Germany is excellent but is probably not the most interesting route. The Automobile Association has suggested routes, times and mileages for journeys throughout Europe (*see www.automobileassociation.com*)

## By Rail

Vilnius is directly linked by rail to the following countries: Latvia, Poland, Ukraine, Belarus, Russia and Kaliningrad, but there is only one route into the Baltics from Western Europe and that is from Warsaw (Poland) to Vilnius. The route from London to Vilnius takes over 45 hours and is much more expensive than flying. The only real advantage of taking the train is if you want to stop off en route and do a bit of exploring. Details of routes and timetables can be found on *www.litrail.lt*

Children enjoying themselves on a boat

**By Sea**

Klaipėda, on the Baltic Sea, is Lithuania's only port. Ferries dock here from various locations in northern Europe. Scandine ferries sail weekly out of Arhus and Kiel in Denmark into Klaipėda. The same line also runs a six times a week service to Klaipėda from Karlshamn, about a 350km drive southwest of Stockholm. Most journeys involve an overnight stay on the boat and work out to be quite expensive if you are also taking a car.

**Timetables**

For up-to-date rail and ferry timetables and routes consult the *Thomas Cook European Rail Timetable*, published monthly, available to buy online at *www.thomascookpublishing.com* or from Thomas Cook branches in the UK, *tel: 01733 416477*.

**Camping**

Camping in the national parks is popular in Lithuania. However, the extreme temperatures in winter restrict camping to summer, late spring and early autumn. It tends to rain a lot in Lithuania so make sure to come prepared. Information is available at the tourist centre of each national park or log on to their individual websites.

**Children**

Children are welcome almost everywhere in Lithuania – cafés, hotels, restaurants and shops. If travelling around Lithuania by car, there are regular service stations with refreshments on the main routes, most of which provide play areas for children.

In the tourist centres the restaurants and cafés are happy to provide children's portions and many have specially designed children's menus. (*See pp152–5 for specific activities.*)

**Climate**

Temperature is generally measured in Celsius. The climate ranges between continental and maritime. Average precipitation is 660mm per annum. Unless you are particularly keen on skiing or skating, spring, summer and autumn are the best times to visit Lithuania. The numerous national and regional parks give the visitor boundless opportunities to appreciate nature and the beauty of the changing seasons throughout the year, but winters can be extremely cold.

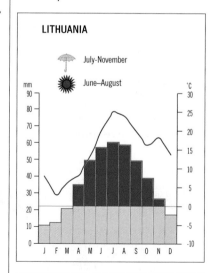

LITHUANIA

July-November

June–August

**Weather Conversion Chart**
25.4mm = 1 inch
°F = 1.8 x °C + 32

## Crime

Vilnius is the third safest city in Eastern and Central Europe, according to the Mercer Human Resource Consulting LLC (*www.imercer.com*). However, normal precautions are advisable and necessary. Be particularly vigilant in bus or train stations and in crowded locations. As in any foreign place, exercise common sense. Take care at night and keep to well-lit relatively busy streets. Do not expose your wallet full of freshly exchanged currency for all to see, walk down deserted streets or leave personal items such as mobile phones or wallets unattended. Try to look like you know what you are doing and where you are going, even if you are lost!

## Customs

As Lithuania is a member of the European Union there are no import restrictions for EU citizens. Non-EU citizens are only entitled to bring in 2 litres of wine, 1 litre of spirits, 200 cigarettes, 250g of tobacco and 50ml perfume.

When leaving the country you can take out as much as you like tax free but there are tax liabilities and procedures to follow on articles over 50 years old. Enquire at the point of sale for details of the paperwork you need to complete.

## Driving

Driving is on the right-hand side of the road, and passing is on the left. Speed

Cheap and reliable and you're carrying a message

Keeping the visitor informed

### Conversion Table

| FROM | TO | MULTIPLY BY |
| --- | --- | --- |
| Inches | Centimetres | 2.54 |
| Feet | Metres | 0.3048 |
| Yards | Metres | 0.9144 |
| Miles | Kilometres | 1.6090 |
| Acres | Hectares | 0.4047 |
| Gallons | Litres | 4.5460 |
| Ounces | Grams | 28.35 |
| Pounds | Grams | 453.6 |
| Pounds | Kilograms | 0.4536 |
| Tons | Tonnes | 1.0160 |

To convert back, for example from centimetres to inches, divide by the number in the third column.

limits are well displayed: 60kph in built-up areas and 90kph on the main roads. On two-lane highways, the speed limit is increased to 130kph from April to September and is 100kph from October to March. Keep a keen eye on speed limits as they change often. Also watch out for hidden police, as what may appear a rural, under-populated area may well still be in an urban speed limit area. The police are armed with speed guns and are not afraid of using them. Fines are levied on the spot.

Seat belts are mandatory and there is a fine of 50lt if you are caught not wearing one.

Petrol is relatively cheap by European standards. Petrol stations are regularly located on the main roads, some open 24 hours, but are much more infrequent in rural areas.

The roads are generally very good on the main routes but can become quite basic in the more rural areas. Ultimately, whether or not you can move with ease around the country depends on the weather. Snow is a major factor here (roadside posts indicate the road margins when snow-covered). The main

### Men's Suits

| | | | | | | | |
| --- | --- | --- | --- | --- | --- | --- | --- |
| UK | 36 | 38 | 40 | 42 | 44 | 46 | 48 |
| Lithuania & Rest of Europe | 46 | 48 | 50 | 52 | 54 | 56 | 58 |
| USA | 36 | 38 | 40 | 42 | 44 | 46 | 48 |

### Dress Sizes

| | | | | | | |
| --- | --- | --- | --- | --- | --- | --- |
| UK | 8 | 10 | 12 | 14 | 16 | 18 |
| France | 36 | 38 | 40 | 42 | 44 | 46 |
| Italy | 38 | 40 | 42 | 44 | 46 | 48 |
| Lithuania & Rest of Europe | 34 | 36 | 38 | 40 | 42 | 44 |
| USA | 6 | 8 | 10 | 12 | 14 | 16 |

### Men's Shirts

| | | | | | | | |
| --- | --- | --- | --- | --- | --- | --- | --- |
| UK | 14 | 14.5 | 15 | 15.5 | 16 | 16.5 | 17 |
| Lithuania & Rest of Europe | 36 | 37 | 38 | 39/40 | 41 | 42 | 43 |
| USA | 14 | 14.5 | 15 | 15.5 | 16 | 16.5 | 17 |

### Men's Shoes

| | | | | | | |
| --- | --- | --- | --- | --- | --- | --- |
| UK | 7 | 7.5 | 8.5 | 9.5 | 10.5 | 11 |
| Lithuania & Rest of Europe | 41 | 42 | 43 | 44 | 45 | 46 |
| USA | 8 | 8.5 | 9.5 | 10.5 | 11.5 | 12 |

### Women's Shoes

| | | | | | | |
| --- | --- | --- | --- | --- | --- | --- |
| UK | 4.5 | 5 | 5.5 | 6 | 6.5 | 7 |
| Lithuania & Rest of Europe | 38 | 38 | 39 | 39 | 40 | 41 |
| USA | 6 | 6.5 | 7 | 7.5 | 8 | 8.5 |

roads are regularly attended to but can still be impassable in extreme conditions. Off these main roads, you may have difficulty and a four-wheel drive would be the minimum requirement to achieve any meaningful level of mobility for touring. It is better to tour in the spring, summer and autumn.

**Car Rental**

All the main international car rental companies have offices in Lithuania. Car rental is generally expensive, with a few local exceptions. Most national and international driving licences are accepted here.

**addCar**
*www.addCarrental.com*

**Altas Rent a Car**
*Tel: (370 612) 944 40. www.altas.lt*

**Avis Car rentals**
*Tel: (370 5) 230 68 20. www.avis.lt*

**Budget Car**
*Tel: (370 5) 230 67 08; email: budget@budget.lt*

**Europcar**
*Tel: (370 5) 212 02 07; email: city@europcar.lt*

**Hertz**
*Tel: (370  5) 272 69 40; email: reservations@hertz.lt*

**Litinterp, Rent a Car**
*Tel: (370  5) 212 38 50 (Vilnius); (370 37) 228 718 (Kaunas); (370  46) 410 644 (Klaipėda); email: Vilnius@litinterp.lt*

**Sixt Rent a Car**
*Tel: (370 5) 239 56 36; www.sixt.lt*

**Unirent Car Rental**
*Tel: (370 700) 558 55; www.unirent.lt*

For emergency road service, telephone *8-800-000-000* or mobile number *1414 188*; *www.motoruras.lt*

A slower but more scenic form of transport

## Embassies and Consulates
### Australia
Vilnius: *Vilniaus g. 23. Tel: (370 5) 212 33 69; e-mail: Australia@consulate.lt*
### Canada
Vilnius: *Jogailos g. 4.*
*Tel: (370 5) 249 09 50;*
*www.canada.lt; e-mail: Vilnius@canada.lt*
### Ireland
*3rd Floor, Business Centre 2000,*
*Jogailos 4. Tel: (370 5) 269 00 44*
*e-mail: ireland.vilnius@gmail.com*
### UK
Vilnius: *Antakalnio g. 2. Tel: (370 5) 246 29 00; www.britain.lt;*
*e-mail: be-vilnius@britain.lt*
### USA
Vilnius: *Akmenų g. 6. Tel: (370 5) 266 55 00; www.usembassy.lt;*
*e-mail: mail@usembassy*

## Emergency telephone numbers
**Ambulance** *03*
**Electrical and Plumbing** *05*
**Fire** *01*
**Gas Service** *04*
**Police** *02*

## Health
There are no immunisation requirements for visiting Lithuania and the health risks generally are negligible. The forest parks and lakes may, at certain times of the year, attract mosquitoes but there is really nothing more sinister than this.

## Insurance
As a member of the European Union the EU health care privileges apply to all EU visitors but there is no harm in taking out additional personal insurance. You can obtain insurance from any travel agent or tour operator in your home country. Most insurance policies should offer adequate cover for medical expenses, theft, loss of baggage or other personal possessions; some policies would extend to cover traveller's cheques and even cash and personal liability. Make sure you check the exclusion clauses, extent and amount of cover. If you have home insurance cover it is worth checking it before you commit to another policy as you may well be covered for some of these eventualities already.

If you are hiring a car, the insurance package usually includes collision damage waiver (CDW) and tends to be compulsory. It is worth checking with your own motor insurance broker what your current policy covers before you leave home. Car hire firms would usually give you the option of paying a certain amount in case of an accident, but the main liability in this event will be yours.

### Great Car Deals
A local firm Add Rent offer cars at half the price of other rental cars. The reason for this is because, as the name suggests, you are advertising something. Your car is advertising Baltic Air and has a destination and a price on a brightly coloured sign sitting on the roof of the car. It makes you somewhat conspicuous but this needs weighing up against the huge saving you are taking advantage of. A relatively new arrival in Lithuania, addCar have branches in Latvia and Estonia. You do have the option of a one-way rental if you fancy touring the Baltic States. There is a charge for dropping it off in another country but again this is competitive.

The disadvantages are that the only car on offer is a 3-door Renault Clio; it has a sign on its roof and you have to pick it up at the airport.

## Language

The national language is Lithuanian. It is one of the oldest Indo-European languages and while close to Latvian it has no similarities with the Slavic languages. There are masculine and female genders in Lithuanian – masculine nouns tend to end with an 's' and female nouns predominantly end with an 'a' or an 'e'. There has been little change in the grammar and vocabulary of Lithuanian over the centuries and some liken it to ancient Sanskrit. It is an unusual language and it is unlikely that you would have heard anything like it before.

## Maps

Tourist offices are a good source of both small and large maps. Each local tourist office will have a supply of maps of the area. Most are free, but when there is a charge, it is a modest one. Petrol stations also sell maps for touring. Bookshops in the main cities also stock a reasonably good supply of maps.

The excellent local guide series *In Your Pocket* include maps in their publications (*see www.inyourpocket.com*)

## Media

The daily English newspapers are *The Baltic Times* and *City Paper,* and in Lithuanian are *Lietuvos rytas, Respubliką, Lietuvos Žinios*. The national public television channel is LT, the largest private channels are LNK, TV3, and BTV. Lithuania's national radio channel is M-1, with M-1 Plius, Radiocentras and News Radio being some of the private broadcasters.

## Medical

The only hospital in Lithuania certified by all major insurance companies is: **Baltic-American Medical and Surgical Clinic** (*Nemencines 54a, Vilnius; tel: (370 5) 234 20 20*). It is a private clinic offering a wide range of western-standard services, including family medicine and dental treatment.

Druskininkai health centre

## PRONUNCIATION

Not as complicated as you might expect. Each letter represents an individual sound and apart from a few exceptions is pronounced exactly as it sounds. A few of the most difficult exceptions are: **c** pronounced **ts** (cats), **j** pronounced like **y** (yesterday), **y** pronounced **i** (hit)

### NUMBERS

| | | |
|---|---|---|
| 1 | vienas (m) | viena(f) |
| 2 | du (m) | dvi (f) |
| 3 | trys | |
| 4 | keturi (m) | keturios (f) |
| 5 | penki (m) | penkios (f) |
| 6 | šeši (m) | šešios (f) |
| 7 | septyni (m) | septynios (f) |
| 8 | aštuoni (m) | aštuonios (f) |
| 9 | devyni (m) | devynios (f) |
| 10 | dešimt | |
| 20 | dvidešimt | |
| 50 | penkiasdešimt | |
| 100 | šimtas | |
| 200 | du šimtai | |

### USEFUL WORDS AND PHRASES

| | |
|---|---|
| Do you speak English? | Ar jus kalbate angliškai? |
| See you | Iki |
| My name is... | Mano vardas… |
| Where is...? | Kur yra…? |
| Hotel | Viešbutis |
| Street | Gatvė |
| Hospital | Ligoninė |
| Chemist | Vaitine |
| Dentist | Dantų gydytojas |
| Bread | Duoną |
| Wine | Vynas |
| Sugar | Cukrus |
| Beer | Alus |
| Coffee | Kava |
| More please | Dar prasui |
| Milk | Pienas |
| Petrol | Benzino |

### POLITE GREETINGS

| | |
|---|---|
| Hello | laba diena |
| Goodbye | viso gero |
| Good morning | labas rytas |
| Good evening | labas vakaras |
| Good night | labanakt |
| Please | prašau, prašom |
| Thank you | ačiū |
| OK | gerai |

### EVERYDAY EXPRESSIONS

| | |
|---|---|
| Yes | taīp |
| No | ne |
| I don't understand | ašnesuprantu |
| Excuse me/sorry | atsiprašau |
| How much? | Kiek kainuoja? |
| Cheap/expensive | pigūs/brangūs |
| Hot/cold | karštas/šaltas |
| Left/right | kaire/dešine |

### TIME

| | |
|---|---|
| Today | šiandien |
| Yesterday | vakar |
| Tomorrow | rytoj |
| In the evening | vakare |

### DAYS OF THE WEEK

| | |
|---|---|
| Monday | Pirmadienis |
| Tuesday | Antradienis |
| Wednesday | Trečiadienis |
| Thursday | Ketvirtadienis |
| Friday | Penktadienis |
| Saturday | Šeštadienis |
| Sunday | Sekmadienis |

Buy a bouquet from the town centre flower shop for birthdays and feastdays

Some others are: **Gedimino Vaistinė** (*Gedimino pr. 27; tel: (370 5) 261 01 35*) open 24 hours, offering essential supplies around the clock in the centre of Vilnius); **Gidenta** (*AVienulio g. 14–3, Vilnius; tel: (370 5) 261 71 43; www.gidenta.lt*); a private dental clinic for all the family; and **Medicine Central Private Clinic** (*Gedimino pr. 1a-19 (second floor), Vilnius; tel: (370 5) 261 35 34; www.clinic.lt*); run by an Australian general practitioner.

## Money Matters
### Currency
The unit of currency in Lithuania is the *Litas* (lt), which has been pegged to the euro at a rate of 3.4528lt = 1 euro, since February 2002. Litas come in note form in 10, 20, 50, 100, 200 and 500 lt. The smaller units are called *centas* (ct) and 100ct = 1lt. The coins come in 1, 2 and 5 lt, and 1, 2, 5, 10, 20 and 50 ct.

### Credit Cards and ATMs
Most restaurants, hotels, cafés and shops accept major credit cards in Lithuania, especially VISA and MasterCard. ATM machines are in abundance in the main cities.

### Exchange
You can only bring a limited amount of litas into Lithuania if you are lucky enough to get hold of any before you arrive, as they are difficult to find. Foreign currencies can easily be exchanged at banks and foreign exchange offices. Traveller's cheques can be changed at the bigger banks. There are also exchange kiosks in the main cities as well as ATM machines. There is an ATM in the arrivals hall at the airport.

## Opening Hours

Work hours are not strictly regulated so those given below may vary. Work hours are sometimes shorter on Fridays and prior to public holidays.

**Government Institutions**
Monday–Friday 8am–5pm
Saturday noon–1pm
**Regular working hours**
Monday–Friday 10am–7pm
Saturday 10am–3pm
**Supermarkets**
They usually operate from 8am–10pm but some stay open until midnight. Some offer 24-hour services. A limited amount of shops open Sunday.

## Organised Tours

**Lithuanian Tours**
*Tel: (370 659) 122 22.*
For organised tours contact the **Vilnius**

**Tourist Information Centre** at the following locations:
*Didžioji g. 31, Vilniaus g. 22 and Gelezinkelio g. 16 (at the railway station); www.vilnius.lt*

## Post Offices (Paštas)

Lithuanian post offices are recognisable by the bright yellow symbol that features the silhouette of an old postal horn. This makes them easy to spot and there are plenty of them. The Central Post Office of Vilnius District is at *Gedimino pr.7; tel: (370 5) 261 67 59.*

**Rates**
Postal rates are dived into two categories, inside Lithuania (1lt) and outside Lithuania (1.7lt), and there is a small difference between postcards and letters.

Find a bargain at a roadside souvenir stall

**Express Mail**

Most international express mail companies are found in Lithuania. These include DHL, EMS, FedEx and UPS. Rates and efficiency vary considerably so check estimated delivery time with each individual company.

**Public Holidays**

**1 January** New Year's Day and National Flag Day.

**16 February** Independence Day.

**11 March** Restoration of Independence.

**March/April** Easter Sunday, Easter Monday.

**1 May** International Labour Day.

**14 June** Day of Mourning and Hope.

**23–24 June** Joninės – the feast of St John – midsummer.

**6 July** Day of Statehood – Crowning of King Mindaugas.

**15 August** Zoline – Feast of the Assumption.

**23 August** Black Ribbon Day (Molotov-Ribbentrop).

**8 September** Crowning of Vytautas the Great.

**25 October** Constitution Day.

**1 November** Vėlinės – All Saints Day.

**25–26 December** Kalėdos – Christmas Day.

**Public Transport**

**By Bus**

This is the most convenient way of getting around the country. Frequent services operate between the main cities and there are also daily or twice-daily

Tourists on a sightseeing outing

The main post office in Kaunas

buses to the remoter regions. There are various bus operators:

**Toks**: (*www.toks.lt*) operates out of Vilnius and **Kautra** (*www.kautra)* is based in Kaunas.

Bus stations (*autobusu stotis*) generally have good clear departure boards. It is best to enquire at the main bus stations for details of rural services, as the smaller towns and villages tend to just have the bus stop sign and no timetables. There are express or regular intercity bus services. Express buses have an 'E' beside them on the timetable, and it is advisable to book a seat in advance in high season as they can fill up very quickly.

**By Ferry**

Ferries operate along the Baltic Coast mainly out of Klaipėda and the only ferry journey you are likely to be taking is from Klaipėda to the Curonian Spit.

**By Rail**

Although cheaper than buses, services on Lithuanian Railways are not as frequent and often not as fast as the buses. The main link between Vilnius and Kaunas has regular commuter trains but the other, longer routes are less well served. Timetables at the stations are not always available, so it is best to consult the website *www.litrail.lt*. See also Timetables p177.

Useful words:

**departure** *isvyksta, isvykimo laikas* or *isvykimas*

**arrival** *atvyksta, atvykimo* or *atvykimas*

## Smoking

Smoking is permitted in almost all public areas. This includes restaurants and bars. However, it is possible to find some smoke-free establishments. The only place smoking is totally prohibited is on public transport.

## Sustainable Tourism

Thomas Cook is a strong advocate of ethical and fairly traded tourism and believes that the travel experience should be as good for the places visited as it is for the people that visit. That's why Thomas Cook is a firm supporter of The Travel Foundation – a charity that develops solutions to help improve and protect holiday destinations, their environment, traditions and culture. To find out what you can do to make a positive difference to the places you travel to and the people who live there, please visit: *www.thetravelfoundation.org.uk*

## Taxis

Rates are variable, according to time and day and whether you pick up a taxi at a rank or flag it down. Drivers are generally obliging, but it is as well to try and establish a fare at the outset. The meters are not always working and you need to make sure you're not being charged night rates during the day. You get the best rate if you call in advance. Wear seat belts if your cab has them. Taxi drivers in Lithuania are not renowned for their patience and caution and often drive at breakneck speed, weaving in and out of traffic.

## Telephones
### Public telephones

Public telephones can be found easily in most cities and towns. You can only make calls on public phones with a call card, which is easy to get – they are sold in press kiosks, supermarkets and post offices. The cards come in a variety of units, ranging from 50 to 200 units.

### Mobile telephones

You can use the roaming facility but this can be expensive. Rates are lowest between midnight and 6am, and highest between 8am and 7pm. Alternatively, if you are planning on making a lot of calls you can buy a prepaid SIM card. The three main Lithuanian mobile

Old style telephone box in Kaunas

companies, Omnitel, Bite and Tele 2, offer prepaid SIM packs to customers.

**Emergency Number**
Dial *112*. No code required.

**National Access Code**
*+ 370*

**Codes for Main Lithuanian Towns**
**Alytus** *(370) 315*
**Birstonas** *(370) 319*
**Druskininkai** *(370) 313*
**Ignalina** *(370) 386*
**Kaunas** *(370) 37*
**Klaipėda** *(370) 46*
**Lazdijai** *(370) 318*
**Marijampole** *(370) 343*
**Molėtai** *(370) 383*
**Neringa** *(370) 469*
**Palanga** *(370) 460*
**Panevėžys** *(370) 45*
**Šiaulių** *(370) 41*
**Trakai** *(370) 528*
**Vilnius** *(370) 5*
**Visaginas** *(370) 386*

**Time and Date**
Local time is GMT + 2 hours, therefore Ireland and the UK are two hours behind. Depending on where you are in the USA and Canada, you will be 7–10 hours behind (10 in California and 7 in New York). Australia and New Zealand are on average 8 hours ahead. The form of writing dates in Lithuanian is: year, month, day (eg, 2006/12/25).

**Tipping**
The more expensive restaurants will include the service charge on the bill. Average tipping in restaurants, if not included, is between 5 per cent and 10 per cent. Generally, in smaller bars and cafés rounding off the bill is sufficient, but of course you are free to reward good service at your discretion.

**Toilets**
There is a shortage of public toilets around Lithuania. They can be found in larger shopping centres, in petrol stations and some tourist offices. If you go into a café to use the toilet, it is a courtesy to leave the small price of a cup of coffee for the attendant. The toilets are generally clean and of the sit-down variety. It is also advisable to carry toilet paper just in case.
M or ^ = Ladies, while V = Gent's room.

**Tourist Offices**
If you find one thing in every city and town in Lithuania, it is a tourist information office. The service they provide is excellent. There is a plethora of information available on accommodation, dining, events, transport, leisure, and anything else you may need.

**Travellers with Disabilities**
Lithuania is fairly up to date on facilities for the disabled traveller, and most public places and modern accommodation are wheelchair accessible. Contact the local tourist offices on arrival for information on what is and what is not accessible, to avoid unnecessary and disappointing journeys. Access to public transport can be difficult, so check this too before setting out.

**ACKNOWLEDGEMENTS**
Thomas Cook Publishing wishes to thank Polly Phillimore, for the photographs in this book, to whom the copyright belongs, except for the following images:

Lithuanian Hydrometeorological Service: page 177
Lithuanian Tourist Board: pages 5, 21, 27, 35, 36, 65, 66a, 75,131, 137, 147, 148, 149, 150, 151, 163, 168, 172, 173
Panevezys Tourist Board: pages 116, 117

# Send your thoughts to
# books@thomascook.com

We're committed to providing the very best up-to-date information in our travel guides and constantly strive to make them as useful as they can be. You can help us to improve future editions by letting us have your feedback. If you've made a wonderful discovery on your travels that we don't already feature, if you'd like to inform us about recent changes to anything that we do include, or if you simply want to let us know your thoughts about this guidebook and how we can make it even better – we'd love to hear from you.

Send us ideas, discoveries and recommendations today and then look out for your valuable input in the next edition of this title. And, as an extra 'thank you' from Thomas Cook Publishing, you'll be automatically entered into our exciting monthly prize draw.

Emails to the above address, or letters to Travellers Project Editor, Thomas Cook Publishing, PO Box 227, Unit 18, Coningsby Road, Peterborough PE3 8SB, UK.

Please don't forget to let us know which title your feedback refers to!

**FOR LABURNUM TECHNOLOGIES**

| | | | |
|---|---|---|---|
| **Design Director** | Alpana Khare | **Designer** | Neeraj Aggarwal |
| **Series Director** | Sunanda Lahiri | **DTP Designer** | Manish Aggarwal |
| **Editor** | Amit Dixit | **Photo Editor** | Manju Singhal |

Thanks to Bikram Grewal for the index.